I0015245

Microsoft Dynamics 365 AI for Business Insights

Transform your business processes with the practical implementation of Dynamics 365 AI modules

Dmitry Shargorodsky

Microsoft Dynamics 365 AI for Business Insights

Copyright © 2024 Packt Publishing

All rights reserved. No part of this book may be reproduced, stored in a retrieval system, or transmitted in any form or by any means, without the prior written permission of the publisher, except in the case of brief quotations embedded in critical articles or reviews.

Every effort has been made in the preparation of this book to ensure the accuracy of the information presented. However, the information contained in this book is sold without warranty, either express or implied. Neither the author, nor Packt Publishing or its dealers and distributors, will be held liable for any damages caused or alleged to have been caused directly or indirectly by this book.

Packt Publishing has endeavored to provide trademark information about all of the companies and products mentioned in this book by the appropriate use of capitals. However, Packt Publishing cannot guarantee the accuracy of this information.

Group Product Manager: Aaron Tanna
Publishing Product Manager: Kushal Dave
Book Project Manager: Manisha Singh
Senior Editor: Nithya Sadanandan
Technical Editor: Vidhisha Patidar
Copy Editor: Safis Editing
Proofreader: Nithya Sadanandan
Indexer: Hemangini Bari
Production Designer: Aparna Bhagat
DevRel Marketing Coordinators: Deepak Kumar and Mayank Singh
Business Development Executive: Saloni Garg

First published: March 2024

Production reference: 1220324

Published by Packt Publishing Ltd.
Grosvenor House
11 St Paul's Square
Birmingham
B3 1RB, UK

ISBN 978-1-80181-094-4

www.packtpub.com

To my wife, Anna, for your love and support as we embark on our many adventures together.
And to our children, who are the light of our lives and the source of our greatest joys.

-- Dmitry Shargorodsky

Contributors

About the author

Dmitry Shargorodsky is a seasoned expert with extensive experience working with Microsoft's Dynamics 365 products since 2004. He has two decades of experience with customer relationship management software, data integration, business intelligence, and now the rapidly developing field of artificial intelligence. Dmitry has honed his skills through hundreds of projects in consulting roles in the areas of education, insurance, investment funds, real estate, legal, manufacturing, wholesale, medical devices, health care, non-profits, software, retail, telecommunications, and others. Leveraging these years of work across many industries, Dmitry incorporates cutting-edge technologies, particularly artificial intelligence tools, to drive innovation and efficiency.

About the reviewer

Umesh Pandit is a seasoned Advisor Solution Architect at DXC Technology, a premier global digital transformation solutions provider. With over 16 years of experience in the IT industry, he specializes in helping organizations translate their strategic business objectives into tangible realities through innovative and scalable solutions leveraging Microsoft technologies.

Passionate about staying at the forefront of emerging technologies, Umesh thrives on continuous learning. He is dedicated to fostering a culture of knowledge exchange within the tech community.

I would like to thank my wife Saroj, and my kids Elina and Aashrut, who encouraged me to follow this passion.

Table of Contents

Part 2: Implementing Dynamics 365 AI Across Business Functions

3

Implementing Dynamics 365 AI for Sales Insights   23

4

Driving Customer Service Excellence with Dynamics 365 AI   33

5

Marketing Optimization with Dynamics 365 AI   43

6

Financial Analytics with Dynamics 365 AI   57

Part 3: Advanced Applications and Future Directions

7

8

"Virtual Agent for Customer Service" in the Context of MS Copilot and Microsoft Dynamics   105

10

Fraud Protection with Dynamics 365 AI   119

Part 4: Looking Ahead

11

Future Trends and Developments in Dynamics 365 AI   137

Preface

Within the dynamic realm of business technology, **artificial intelligence** (**AI**) stands as a pivotal force, revolutionizing company operations, decision-making processes, and customer interactions. Central to this transformative wave is Microsoft Dynamics 365 AI, which presents a comprehensive array of tools that seamlessly incorporate the extensive potential of AI into routine business activities. This suite enables businesses, regardless of their size, to harness the power of advanced analytics, predictive insights, and intelligent automation, bringing sophistication and efficiency to their operations.

The book will provide a comprehensive exploration of Dynamics 365 AI, from foundational concepts and architecture to specific applications across sales, customer service, marketing, and finance. It delves into implementing generative AI, optimizing operations with Microsoft 365 Copilot, and employing AI-driven strategies for fraud protection. The book concludes with a forward-looking perspective on emerging trends and future developments in business AI solutions.

Who this book is for

This book is crafted for a broad audience, ranging from IT professionals and data scientists to business analysts and decision-makers interested in harnessing the power of AI within their operations. Whether you are a Dynamics 365 developer looking to deepen your understanding of its AI capabilities, a business executive aiming to leverage AI for competitive advantage, or an IT student eager to explore the practical applications of AI in the business world, this book offers valuable insights and guidance.

What this book covers

Chapter 1, Introduction and Architectural Overview of Dynamics 365 AI, provides an overview of Dynamics 365 AI, discussing its significance in the modern business landscape and how it integrates artificial intelligence to transform various business functions.

Chapter 2, Microsoft Dynamics 365 AI Architecture and Foundations, is an exploration of the underlying architecture of Dynamics 365 AI, detailing the key components, their interactions, and the foundational technology that powers the AI capabilities within Dynamics 365.

Chapter 3, Implementing Dynamics 365 AI for Sales Insights, focuses on leveraging Dynamics 365 AI for enhancing sales processes, including customer segmentation, lead scoring, and personalized sales strategies, to drive revenue and improve sales efficiency.

Chapter 4, Driving Customer Service Excellence with Dynamics 365 AI, examines how Dynamics 365 AI can transform customer service, utilizing virtual agents, sentiment analysis, and intelligent case routing to enhance customer interactions and satisfaction.

Chapter 5, Marketing Optimization with Dynamics 365 AI, discusses the application of Dynamics 365 AI in marketing, highlighting how AI-driven customer insights, content personalization, and campaign optimization can elevate marketing strategies.

Chapter 6, Financial Analytics with Dynamics 365 AI, explores the use of Dynamics 365 AI in financial analytics, covering AI-powered forecasting, budgeting, fraud detection, and risk management to bolster financial decision-making and security.

Chapter 7, Leveraging Generative AI in Dynamics 365, delves into the integration and applications of generative AI within Dynamics 365, showcasing how businesses can use generative models for content creation, code generation, and more innovative solutions.

Chapter 8, Harnessing MS Copilot for Enhanced Business Insights , takes an in-depth look at MS Copilot and its features, emphasizing how its integration enhances business intelligence, data analysis, and operational efficiency across Dynamics 365 applications.

Chapter 9, "Virtual Agent for Customer Service" in the Context of MS Copilot and Microsoft Dynamics, explores the deployment of AI-driven virtual agents within Dynamics 365 for automated customer support, focusing on implementation strategies, customization, and real-world success stories.

Chapter 10, Fraud Protection with Dynamics 365 AI, addresses how Dynamics 365 AI can be utilized for advanced fraud detection and prevention, outlining strategic approaches, technologies, and case studies in mitigating fraud-related risks.

Chapter 11, Future Trends and Developments in Dynamics 365 AI, foretells the emerging trends and future developments in Dynamics 365 AI, contemplating the evolution of AI technologies and their implications for businesses leveraging Dynamics 365.

> **Note**
> This book has been created by authors, technical experts, and a professional publishing team. We use many tools, including cutting-edge AI such as ChatGPT, to create the best possible material for our readers to help them on their IT journey.

To get the most out of this book

Readers looking to fully benefit from this guide should have a basic acquaintance with Microsoft Dynamics 365 and its application in business operations. While specific technical expertise in AI programming or data science is not necessary, a curiosity about artificial intelligence and its potential to solve complex business issues will serve to enhance the reader's engagement with the material.

An openness to absorbing technical content is encouraged, as it will aid in fully understanding the implementation strategies discussed.

By focusing on actionable insights and offering clear guidance, this book aims to enable readers to effectively employ Dynamics 365 AI within their organizations. The ultimate objective is to foster operational efficiency, drive innovation, and secure a strategic advantage by leveraging the power of AI.

Conventions used

There are a number of text conventions used throughout this book.

Bold: Indicates a new term, an important word, or words that you see onscreen. For instance, words in menus or dialog boxes appear in **bold**. Here is an example: "Select **System info** from the **Administration** panel."

> **Tips or important notes**
> Appear like this.

Get in touch

Feedback from our readers is always welcome.

General feedback: If you have questions about any aspect of this book, email us at customercare@ packtpub.com and mention the book title in the subject of your message.

Errata: Although we have taken every care to ensure the accuracy of our content, mistakes do happen. If you have found a mistake in this book, we would be grateful if you would report this to us. Please visit www.packtpub.com/support/errata and fill in the form.

Piracy: If you come across any illegal copies of our works in any form on the internet, we would be grateful if you would provide us with the location address or website name. Please contact us at copyright@packt.com with a link to the material.

If you are interested in becoming an author: If there is a topic that you have expertise in and you are interested in either writing or contributing to a book, please visit authors.packtpub.com.

Share Your Thoughts

Once you've read *Microsoft Dynamics 365 AI for Business Insights*, we'd love to hear your thoughts! Scan the QR code below to go straight to the Amazon review page for this book and share your feedback.

https://packt.link/r/180181094X

Your review is important to us and the tech community and will help us make sure we're delivering excellent quality content.

Download a free PDF copy of this book

Thanks for purchasing this book!

Do you like to read on the go but are unable to carry your print books everywhere?

Is your eBook purchase not compatible with the device of your choice?

Don't worry, now with every Packt book you get a DRM-free PDF version of that book at no cost.

Read anywhere, any place, on any device. Search, copy, and paste code from your favorite technical books directly into your application.

The perks don't stop there, you can get exclusive access to discounts, newsletters, and great free content in your inbox daily

Follow these simple steps to get the benefits:

1. Scan the QR code or visit the link below

https://packt.link/free-ebook/978-1-80181-094-4

2. Submit your proof of purchase
3. That's it! We'll send your free PDF and other benefits to your email directly

Part 1:
Foundations of
Dynamics 365 AI

Welcome to the foundational journey into the world of Dynamics 365 AI, an integrated suite designed by Microsoft to bring the transformative power of artificial intelligence directly into the hands of businesses. This initial segment of our book lays the groundwork for understanding the core principles, technologies, and architectures that underpin Dynamics 365 AI. It is here that we embark on an exploratory path, aimed at demystifying AI within the Dynamics 365 environment and illustrating how it serves as a pivotal tool in enhancing and streamlining business processes.

This part has the following chapters:

- *Chapter 1, Introduction and Architectural Overview of Dynamics 365 AI*
- *Chapter 2, Microsoft Dynamics 365 AI Architecture and Foundations*

Introduction and Architectural Overview of Dynamics 365 AI

Welcome to the first chapter of this comprehensive guide on Microsoft Dynamics 365 AI for Business Insights. As businesses increasingly adopt data-driven approaches to gain a competitive edge, the need for intelligent tools has never been more acute. Microsoft's Dynamics 365 AI platform serves as a cornerstone in this digital transformation journey, offering scalable, versatile, and insightful solutions. However, before we delve into the practical applications across various business modules such as sales, marketing, customer service, and financial analytics, it's crucial to understand the architectural foundation that makes all of this possible.

This opening chapter provides an overview of Dynamics 365 AI, breaking down its key features, benefits, and the business problems it aims to solve. The reader will gain a solid understanding of how this robust AI solution integrates with the Dynamics 365 suite, enhancing functionality and enabling intelligent decision-making processes. We'll explore the core architectural elements that lend the platform its flexibility and power, setting the stage for subsequent chapters that will dive into each specialized module in detail.

In this chapter, we will cover the following main topics:

- The importance of data-driven insights in business

- An overview of Microsoft Dynamics 365 AI for Business Insights

- The objectives and structure of the book

By the end of this chapter, you'll be well-equipped with the foundational knowledge needed to appreciate the capabilities of Dynamics 365 AI. This understanding is essential not just for IT professionals and decision-makers but for anyone interested in leveraging AI for business excellence. So, let's embark on this educational journey and unveil what makes Dynamics 365 AI a game-changing tool in the modern business landscape.

Why artificial intelligence?

In an age defined by technological prowess and digital transformation, the amalgamation of **artificial intelligence** (**AI**) with enterprise software solutions has emerged as a non-negotiable for businesses seeking to maintain a competitive edge. Recognizing this, Microsoft, a titan in technological innovation, unveiled Dynamics 365 AI. This groundbreaking artificial intelligence system effortlessly complements the already formidable Dynamics 365 suite. Through this integration, businesses gain the leverage to tap into AI's immense potential, radically revamping their operational paradigms.

The inaugural chapter embarks on a journey through the labyrinthine world of Dynamics 365 AI, meticulously dissecting its myriad features, advantages, and the specific business challenges it's designed to address. What becomes evident is that Dynamics 365 AI is not merely an add-on or an ancillary tool; it's an intricate instrument woven into the fabric of the existing Dynamics 365 modules. This strategic design facilitates businesses in deriving AI-driven insights directly within their established workflows, effectively eradicating the chasm that often exists between raw data analytics and tangible, actionable insights.

One salient attribute of Dynamics 365 AI lies in its prowess to endow organizations with data-powered decision-making faculties. Traditional data analytics paradigms, albeit effective, often lean heavily on manual interpretation and prolonged timelines. Contrarily, Dynamics 365 AI serves as a catalyst, ushering in an era where data undergoes swift processing and precise interpretation and is metamorphosed into actionable directives. This agility ensures that businesses remain nimble, responding to fluctuating landscapes in real time and seizing emerging opportunities.

Dynamics 365 AI's horizons extend far beyond rudimentary data analysis. This powerhouse encapsulates a gamut of AI functionalities, spanning the realms of virtual agents, granular customer insights, predictive market analytics, and automated service provisions. Organizations, regardless of their operational niches, find themselves armed with tools and insights tailored to optimize sales trajectories, amplify customer engagement metrics, and proactively discern market oscillations.

At its foundation, Dynamics 365 AI revolutionizes customer engagement. With a hyper-focus on customer centricity, the platform empowers businesses to understand their clientele better. Through advanced AI-driven tools, companies can now anticipate customer needs, predict future behaviors, and proactively address potential pain points, cultivating an environment of trust and loyalty.

The sales dimension, too, receives a significant uplift. Gone are the days of speculative sales strategies. Dynamics 365 AI introduces a data-backed approach, allowing sales teams to prioritize leads based on intelligent insights, nurture potential clients more effectively, and optimize the sales funnel for enhanced conversions.

On the marketing front, the integration of AI means a more targeted and efficient strategy. By analyzing vast datasets, Dynamics 365 AI can segment audiences, predict campaign effectiveness, and provide recommendations on optimizing marketing spend. These insights enable marketers to craft campaigns that resonate deeply with their target demographics.

Beyond customer engagement, sales, and marketing, the platform also addresses operational efficiencies. Service automation, fraud detection, and predictive maintenance become integral components of the Dynamics 365 AI ecosystem. By proactively identifying potential operational bottlenecks and security threats, businesses can ensure uninterrupted, efficient, and secure operations.

In wrapping up this initial exploration, it becomes irrefutably clear that as the digital landscape continues to evolve, tools such as Dynamics 365 AI will transition from being beneficial to absolutely vital. Microsoft's genius lies in weaving AI's potential within the trusted framework of Dynamics 365, allowing businesses of all scales and sectors to seamlessly embrace the AI revolution.

As readers delve deeper into the forthcoming chapters, they'll be equipped with a holistic understanding of Dynamics 365 AI's transformative potential, ready to harness its power to redefine their organizational trajectories.

The importance of data-driven insights in business

In the modern business landscape, data reigns supreme. Often termed the **oil of the digital age**, data has the unparalleled potential to drive businesses forward, fueling growth, innovation, and competitiveness. However, raw data, in its untamed form, offers little value. It's the insights derived from this data that transform it into a powerful tool, enabling businesses to make informed decisions, understand their markets, and ultimately thrive.

Historically, businesses primarily relied on intuition, past experiences, and occasionally a bit of calculated risk-taking to navigate their trajectories. While these factors remain important, they no longer suffice in isolation. In our intricate, fast-paced digital era, being equipped with data-driven insights has transitioned from a luxury to a fundamental necessity. It is these insights that facilitate a deeper understanding of market dynamics, customer behaviors, operational efficiencies, and emerging trends.

One of the paramount advantages of embracing data-driven insights is the ability to better understand customers. In an age where customer preferences are constantly evolving, businesses can no longer afford to make assumptions. Through data analytics, businesses can gain a clear picture of who their customers are, what they desire, their purchasing habits, and their pain points. This knowledge ensures that companies can tailor their offerings, creating products and services that genuinely resonate with their target audience.

Furthermore, data-driven insights provide businesses with a competitive edge. In saturated markets where multiple brands vie for consumer attention, having in-depth knowledge can be the determining factor between leading the pack or lagging. By harnessing the power of data, businesses can identify gaps in the market, predict emerging trends, and adapt rapidly to shifts, ensuring they stay ahead of competitors.

Operational efficiency is another realm significantly enhanced by data insights. Traditional methods often involve a certain level of trial and error, resulting in wasted resources and time. However, with actionable insights derived from data, businesses can streamline their operations, identifying bottlenecks, optimizing processes, and making informed decisions that directly impact the bottom line.

Financial health, undeniably crucial for any business, also stands to benefit from a data-centric approach. Data analytics can illuminate patterns, revealing areas of unnecessary expenditure, potential investment opportunities, or segments of the business that demand financial attention. Thus, companies are better positioned to allocate resources effectively, ensuring financial stability and growth.

The rise of global markets also underscores the need for data-driven insights. As businesses expand beyond local and national borders, understanding diverse markets, each with its unique dynamics, becomes paramount. Data provides these insights, allowing companies to tailor strategies for different regions, ensuring optimal market penetration and brand resonance.

Moreover, in an age of rapid technological advancement, product development and innovation are pivotal. Here, too, data plays a crucial role. By understanding what features customers appreciate, which ones they don't, and what they wish to see in future iterations, businesses can design products that not only meet but exceed customer expectations.

Risk management, an integral aspect of any business strategy, is substantially enhanced by data insights. Predictive analytics can forewarn businesses about potential risks, whether they're operational, financial, or market-related. When armed with this knowledge, businesses can devise strategies to mitigate these risks or, in some cases, avoid them altogether.

In the realm of marketing, the shift from generic to personalized campaigns has been facilitated by data-driven insights. Understanding consumer behavior, preferences, and trends enables marketers to craft campaigns that resonate on a personal level, increasing engagement and conversion rates.

It's worth noting, however, that with great power comes great responsibility. As businesses harness the potential of data, ethical considerations around data privacy and security become paramount. Ensuring that data collection and analysis are conducted ethically and transparently is vital not just for legal compliance but also for maintaining customer trust.

In conclusion, as we forge ahead into an increasingly data-centric future, the importance of data-driven insights in business cannot be overstated. From enhancing operational efficiency to crafting personalized marketing campaigns, data is the catalyst propelling businesses toward unprecedented growth and success. Those who embrace its potential stand to lead, and those who don't risk being left behind.

An overview of Microsoft Dynamics 365 AI for Business Insights

Microsoft Dynamics 365, a comprehensive suite of business applications, has consistently evolved to address the multifaceted needs of modern businesses. Central to its evolution has been its integration with AI, creating **Dynamics 365 AI**. This integration signifies Microsoft's commitment to providing businesses with tools that harness the power of data and turn it into actionable insights.

At its core, Dynamics 365 AI is designed to bring intelligence into business processes, eliminating manual tasks and providing predictions based on organizational data. This is more than just an augmentation; it's a transformative process that revitalizes how businesses operate, enhancing efficiency and strategic decision-making.

One of the most salient features of Dynamics 365 AI is its ability to seamlessly work in tandem with other Dynamics 365 apps. This synergy ensures a holistic approach where AI-driven insights are not siloed but are accessible and usable across all business functionalities. Whether it's sales, customer service, or marketing, Dynamics 365 AI ensures that every decision is underpinned by robust data insights.

Furthermore, Dynamics 365 AI is not a rigid, one-size-fits-all solution. Recognizing the diversity of business needs and operations, Microsoft has designed it to be modular, as can be seen in the following list. This means businesses can choose specific AI-driven functionalities pertinent to their operational needs, ensuring flexibility and relevance:

- **Sales Insights**, one of the prominent modules, leverages AI to empower sales teams. With features such as predictive lead scoring and next-best-action suggestions, salespeople are equipped to focus on high-potential leads and navigate the sales process more efficiently. The AI doesn't just highlight potential leads; it provides a roadmap on how to approach them, taking into account historical data and patterns.

- **Customer Service Insights** is another transformative module. Here, Dynamics 365 AI analyses customer interactions and feedback to offer insights into customer satisfaction and areas of improvement. This can range from understanding common pain points to predicting when a customer might churn. By being proactive rather than reactive, businesses can enhance customer satisfaction significantly.

- **Marketing Insights** takes the guesswork out of marketing campaigns. Instead of generalized campaigns, Dynamics 365 AI analyses customer data to allow for hyper-targeted marketing efforts. Whether it's understanding which demographic responds best to a particular marketing channel or predicting emerging market trends, AI ensures that every marketing decision is data-backed.

- **Financial Insights** is a testament to the versatility of Dynamics 365 AI. By going beyond customer-facing operations, this module dives deep into a company's financial data. It aids in predicting cash flow trends, assessing financial risks, and even detecting anomalies that could indicate fraud. Thus, businesses can ensure financial stability and make informed investment decisions.

Yet, Dynamics 365 AI is not just about individual modules. It's about interconnectivity. The AI has the ability to cross-reference data from various sources, ensuring a 360-degree view of operations. For instance, insights from the sales module can influence marketing strategies, creating a cohesive, unified approach to business growth.

Another notable feature is the integration with tools such as Power BI. This means that the insights generated by Dynamics 365 AI can be visualized in detailed, intuitive dashboards. Decision-makers no longer need to sift through pages of raw data. Instead, they're presented with clear, visual representations that allow for instant understanding and swift decision-making.

The adaptability of Dynamics 365 AI is further exemplified by its learning capabilities. It's not just about providing insights based on existing data; the AI is continually learning. As more data flows in, the AI refines its models, ensuring that the insights remain relevant, timely, and increasingly accurate.

Moreover, Microsoft ensures that deploying these AI functionalities doesn't require a Ph.D. in artificial intelligence. With user-friendly interfaces and guided processes, businesses can integrate AI into their operations without a steep learning curve.

In terms of security and compliance, Microsoft has taken extensive measures to ensure that Dynamics 365 AI adheres to global standards. Data privacy, especially when integrated with AI, is paramount, and Microsoft ensures that businesses can leverage the power of AI without compromising on data integrity.

In conclusion, Microsoft Dynamics 365 AI for Business Insights is not just a supplementary tool; it's a game-changer. By weaving AI into the fabric of business operations, Microsoft is ensuring that businesses are not just surviving in the modern landscape but thriving, powered by data-driven insights that catalyze growth, efficiency, and innovation.

The objectives and structure of the book

The digital revolution has spurred businesses to integrate technology into their core strategies. However, merely collecting data is not sufficient; understanding and deriving insights from this data is paramount. Recognizing this need, this book endeavors to guide readers through the transformative power of Microsoft Dynamics 365 AI for Business Insights. The objective is not just to provide an overview but to delve deep, offering insights into its multifaceted capabilities and demonstrating how it can be harnessed to drive a business forward in an increasingly competitive market.

This primary goal of this book is to unveil the capabilities of Dynamics 365 AI in providing actionable business insights. We aim to shed light on the symbiotic relationship between the Dynamics 365 suite and its AI capabilities. Through the subsequent chapters, the reader will grasp how this robust tool, when interwoven with the vast functionalities of Dynamics 365, can drive intelligent decision-making processes, thereby elevating business operations to unprecedented heights. Our approach is not just theoretical; it's designed to be eminently practical, with real-world examples and case studies that showcase the tool's tangible impact in real business environments.

Structure is paramount for clarity, and this book has been meticulously crafted to offer readers a logical, step-by-step journey through Dynamics 365 AI. Beginning with an introductory overview, we set the stage, ensuring every reader, regardless of their prior knowledge, has a foundational understanding upon which to build. This foundation is crucial because the subsequent sections delve deeper, exploring individual modules such as Sales Insights, Customer Service Insights, Marketing

Insights, and more. Each module will be unpacked in detail, highlighting its unique features, benefits, and implementation strategies.

Another pivotal objective of this book is to address the game-changing advancements in generative AI. With technology evolving at a dizzying pace, it's essential for businesses to stay updated with the latest developments. As such, dedicated sections of the book are committed to discussing the integration of OpenAI, Azure Open AI service, ChatGPT, and MS Copilot within the Dynamics 365 AI ecosystem. This inclusion ensures readers are equipped with the knowledge of cutting-edge tools and strategies, ready to implement them for enhanced business outcomes.

While understanding the functionalities of Dynamics 365 AI is essential, it's equally crucial to recognize its practical applications across varied industries. To this end, the book incorporates diverse case studies. These real-world examples provide readers with a lens through which they can visualize the tangible impacts of implementing Dynamics 365 AI solutions in their own businesses or organizations. Each case study has been chosen to represent a range of industries, ensuring broad applicability and relevance.

The overarching objective, however, remains consistent: empowerment. By the time readers turn the last page, they should not only possess an in-depth understanding of Dynamics 365 AI but feel confident in their ability to implement its solutions tailored to their business needs. They will be equipped to leverage AI's prowess to make intelligent, data-driven decisions that propel their businesses into the future.

Furthermore, as we navigate through the chapters, the structure of the book facilitates a holistic understanding, bridging the gap between technical know-how and strategic implementation. We touch upon the challenges businesses may encounter when integrating AI-driven insights into their operations and provide strategies to overcome these hurdles. By doing so, the book serves as both a comprehensive guide and a practical manual, offering readers the theoretical knowledge and actionable steps required to harness the full potential of Dynamics 365 AI.

In conclusion, the essence of this book lies in its balanced blend of depth and breadth, theory and practice, strategy and action. Through its structured approach, it aims to be an essential companion for businesses, professionals, and enthusiasts eager to ride the wave of AI-driven insights, optimizing their strategies and operations for the challenges and opportunities of the modern business landscape.

Summary

In this introductory chapter, the focus was on providing a holistic understanding of Microsoft's Dynamics 365 AI for Business Insights. The chapter starts by underlining the growing importance of data-driven strategies in today's competitive business landscape. It introduced Dynamics 365 AI as a cornerstone for digital transformation, detailing its key features, advantages, and the various business challenges it aims to address.

An in-depth look into the architecture of Dynamics 365 AI was provided, highlighting how it integrates seamlessly with the broader Dynamics 365 suite to enhance functionalities and facilitate intelligent decision-making. The objective is to equip the reader with the foundational knowledge needed to navigate the subsequent specialized modules discussed in the following chapters. By the end, you should have a solid grasp of what makes Dynamics 365 AI a powerful tool for modern businesses. In the next chapter, we will address Microsoft Dynamics 365 AI's architecture and foundational elements.

Questions

1. What are the primary benefits of integrating Dynamics 365 AI into the broader Dynamics 365 ecosystem?

2. How does the cloud-based nature of Dynamics 365 AI contribute to its scalability?

3. What are some key features that make Dynamics 365 AI's architecture sophisticated and robust?

4. Why is it important to have a well-rounded understanding of the architectural aspects of Dynamics 365 AI before diving into its specific modules?

Answers

1. The primary benefits of integration include enhanced functionality across CRM, ERP, and other specialized applications. The integration allows for seamless scalability, real-time data analysis, and intelligent decision-making capabilities.

2. Being cloud-based means that Dynamics 365 AI can easily adapt to growing data volumes and computational needs without requiring significant hardware investment. This facilitates the easy scaling of business operations and data analytics capabilities.

3. Some key features include its cloud-based structure, real-time data analytics, continuous learning capabilities, and seamless integration with existing Dynamics 365 modules and other Microsoft services.

4. A well-rounded understanding of the architecture helps to appreciate how the specific modules function and integrate with each other . It provides context for how the AI capabilities are built to be modular yet cohesive, thereby enabling more effective and intelligent business operations.

Microsoft Dynamics 365 AI Architecture and Foundations

Welcome to *Chapter 2*, where we will delve into the technical depths of Microsoft Dynamics 365 AI's architecture and foundational elements. By building upon the broad understanding acquired from the first chapter, it's time to investigate the structural components that make this platform both versatile and powerful. This chapter aims to clarify how Dynamics 365 AI is engineered and how its various elements come together to provide a cohesive, intelligent business solution.

We will cover the following main topics:

- An overview of the architecture of Microsoft Dynamics 365 AI
- The key components and their interactions
- Integration considerations and best practices

The first section, *An overview of the architecture of Microsoft Dynamics 365 AI*, serves as a detailed introduction to the core framework that enables Dynamics 365 AI to function effectively. We will explore the cloud-based architecture, its modularity, and how it's designed for scalability and flexibility. This foundation will help you better understand how the platform offers both specific and integrated solutions for a wide range of business applications.

Following this, we move on to the second section, *The key components and their interactions*, where we dissect the essential parts of Dynamics 365 AI. We will talk about the various modules and functionalities, their interdependencies, and how they interact to create a seamless AI-driven experience. Whether it's data analytics, predictive algorithms, or customer engagement tools, understanding these interactions is vital for leveraging the platform's full potential.

Concluding the chapter, the *Integration considerations and best practices* section will provide practical advice on how to best integrate Dynamics 365 AI into your existing systems. Here, we will look at the typical challenges that organizations face during integration and share expert guidance on overcoming these obstacles. From data migration to software compatibility and security considerations, this section will prepare you for a smooth and efficient implementation process.

By the end of this chapter, you should have a robust understanding of the architecture and foundational elements of Dynamics 365 AI, arming you with the knowledge you need to implement and optimize this powerful tool in your own business environment.

An overview of the architecture of Microsoft Dynamics 365 AI

Understanding the architecture of Microsoft Dynamics 365 AI is akin to unlocking the blueprints of a remarkably complex machine. By analyzing its individual parts, how they are connected, and their designated functions, we can comprehend how the machine works as a whole. Such an understanding is crucial, especially for business leaders, IT professionals, and solution architects who are planning to leverage the full capabilities of this platform. This section provides a detailed examination of the underlying technical structure and components that constitute the Dynamics 365 AI platform.

The following image provides an illustrated overview:

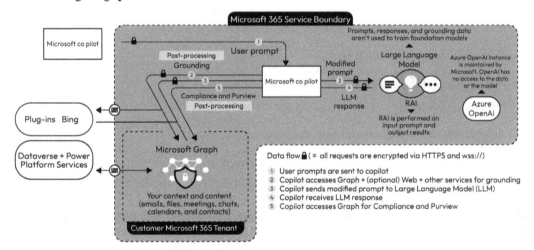

Figure 2.1 – Overview of the architecture

Cloud-based architecture

At the core of Dynamics 365 AI is cloud-based architecture, which allows the platform to benefit from the scalability, flexibility, and ease of access that come with cloud computing. This model facilitates a quicker deployment process, minimizes infrastructure costs, and enables seamless integration with other cloud services. Given the nature of AI, which often requires significant computational power, being cloud-native allows Dynamics 365 AI to harness resources on-demand, thereby efficiently handling large-scale data processing and machine learning tasks.

AI technologies integration

A distinguishing factor of Dynamics 365 AI is its seamless integration of various AI technologies, such as machine learning, **natural language processing** (**NLP**), and cognitive services. Machine learning models power the analytics and predictive capabilities of the system, enabling data-driven insights. NLP allows for intelligent interactions with users, enhancing chatbot functionalities and virtual agents. Cognitive services, which encompass computer vision and other AI capabilities, add another layer of intelligence to the system, further enabling businesses to gather and interpret data across various touchpoints.

Modular components and microservices

The architecture is designed in a modular fashion, with discrete components and services that are built to perform specific tasks yet can interact and integrate seamlessly. This modular design follows the microservices architecture pattern, which ensures that each component is loosely coupled, independently deployable, and organized around specific business capabilities. Such a structure not only makes it easier to customize the system according to specific business needs but also enhances the maintainability and scalability of the entire platform.

Data management and storage

Dynamics 365 AI leverages Microsoft's Azure Data Lake for scalable and secure data storage solutions. This ensures the platform can manage vast amounts of structured and unstructured data, a critical requirement given the data-intensive nature of AI algorithms. Azure Data Lake is designed for high-speed data analytics, making it an ideal match for the real-time analysis requirements of Dynamics 365 AI.

Security and compliance

With data being the new oil, securing it is paramount. The Dynamics 365 AI platform incorporates robust security measures that are aligned with Microsoft's stringent compliance standards. Encryption protocols, access controls, and constant monitoring are some of the built-in features that ensure data integrity and confidentiality.

API and SDKs

Dynamics 365 AI offers a set of APIs and SDKs to enable customizations and integrations with other platforms and services. This flexibility is essential for businesses that may already have a tech stack in place or unique requirements that go beyond the out-of-box functionalities.

Real-time analytics engine

Another pivotal component is the real-time analytics engine, designed to offer immediate insights and facilitate quick decision-making. This engine is optimized to perform complex computations in real time, translating into actionable insights that businesses can leverage instantly.

Streamlined user interface

One must not overlook the significance of the user interface in the architecture. The Dynamics 365 AI dashboard is intuitively designed to present complex data analytics in an understandable manner, ensuring that users can easily interact with the system and extract the insights they need.

Infrastructure resilience and fault tolerance

The platform, built with resilience in mind, has features for automatic failover, load balancing, and disaster recovery. This ensures that the Dynamics 365 AI system is not just powerful but also reliable, a crucial consideration for businesses aiming for continuous operation.

Extensibility and future-proofing

Lastly, the architecture is built to be extensible and capable of incorporating future advancements in AI and machine learning. As the technology landscape evolves, the Dynamics 365 AI platform is geared to adapt, ensuring a future-proof solution that can meet emerging business challenges head-on.

To sum it up, the architecture of Dynamics 365 AI is a meticulously designed system that integrates multiple AI technologies and business modules to deliver a robust, scalable, and intelligent business solution. It stands as a paragon of how architectural sophistication can enable the practical application of AI in solving real-world business problems. This comprehensive understanding should equip you with the foundational knowledge to explore how these elements work together to deliver powerful business insights and drive intelligent decision-making processes.

The key components and their interactions

While understanding the broader architecture of Dynamics 365 AI sets the stage, delving into the essential components and their interactions takes us a level deeper into the operational mechanics of this remarkable platform. These components include data storage, AI models, cognitive services, and integration interfaces. In this section, we will explore how these parts communicate, collaborate, and work in concert to enable machine learning, advanced analytics, and intelligent automation within the business ecosystem.

Data storage – the bedrock of AI

Data storage in Dynamics 365 AI is facilitated through Microsoft's **Azure Data Lake**, a scalable and secure cloud-based repository designed for data analytics. However, it's not just a place to dump your data; it's an active component that interacts with other parts of the system. The Azure Data Lake serves as the foundational layer where raw data is ingested from various sources, including IoT devices, CRM systems, and even external APIs. Once ingested, the data are then pre-processed and made ready for further analysis. Data storage is not a passive repository but an active participant that communicates with other components, such as AI models, to facilitate real-time analytics and predictive insights.

AI models – the analytical engines

At the heart of Dynamics 365 AI's capabilities are its various machine learning models. These models take the processed data from Azure Data Lake and run a series of computations to generate actionable insights. These might range from predictive maintenance schedules in a manufacturing setup to customer behavior analysis in a retail environment. The AI models are trained to interpret complex patterns in the data, and their outputs are then sent to other components, such as dashboards or third-party apps, via APIs. The models continuously learn from new data, adapting and optimizing their algorithms for better future predictions, making them the dynamic, ever-improving engines of the system.

Cognitive services – adding a layer of intelligence

Microsoft's **Cognitive Services** play a crucial role in enhancing Dynamics 365 AI functionalities. These are a collection of pre-built algorithms and models that add capabilities such as natural language processing, computer vision, and sentiment analysis. For instance, a customer service chatbot can understand user queries more effectively by using the language-understanding service, while sentiment analysis can help gauge customer satisfaction levels. These services interact closely with both data storage and AI models, as they often need access to large sets of data to function optimally and may also require the analytical capabilities of AI models for more complex tasks.

Integration interfaces – the connective tissue

In any sophisticated system, seamless integration between different components is crucial. Dynamics 365 AI achieves this through a robust set of APIs and SDKs, which serve as the interaction layer between its native components and external systems. This allows businesses to integrate Dynamics 365 AI into their existing tech stack or even extend its capabilities by connecting it to specialized third-party services. Whether it's pulling data from an ERP system into the Azure Data Lake or pushing analytical insights into an external business intelligence tool, the integration interfaces make it happen smoothly. These APIs and SDKs are designed to be secure and fast, providing a reliable channel for component interaction.

Cross-component collaboration – a symphony of interactions

So, how do these components work together? Imagine a scenario where a retail business wants to predict future sales trends. Raw sales data from the POS system are stored in the Azure Data Lake. AI models analyze this data to identify patterns and trends, aided by Cognitive Services that may add layers of interpretation, such as customer sentiment. Once the analysis is complete, the insights are made available to decision-makers through the dashboard or sent to an external BI tool via APIs. In this entire journey, each component has a role to play, and it's their well-co-ordinated interaction that brings about the end result.

Business empowerment – the ultimate goal

The amalgamation of these components aims to provide businesses with the tools they need to be more data-driven, efficient, and intelligent. With such a sophisticated array of components working in unison, businesses can extract valuable insights, improve operational efficiencies, and ultimately make better decisions. This composite view can help businesses optimize various aspects, from supply chain management to customer relations, thus offering a competitive edge in today's data-driven marketplace.

Scalability and adaptability – designed for growth

Because each of these components operates in a cloud-based, modular environment, scaling up or adapting to new business needs is remarkably easy. Need to add more data storage or incorporate new machine learning models? The architecture allows for such adjustments without causing disruptions, making sure that as your business grows, so do your Dynamics 365 AI capabilities.

Security and compliance across components

Given that data is coursing through multiple components, from storage to AI models, maintaining a high level of security and compliance is critical. Microsoft ensures that data is encrypted during transit and at rest, and robust authentication protocols are in place for APIs and SDKs. This cross-component security ensures the integrity and confidentiality of business-critical data.

Lastly, it's worth noting that Microsoft's commitment to AI and cloud computing translates into regular updates and improvements across all these components. New machine learning models, enhancements to Cognitive Services, or updates to the APIs can appear as part of their update cycle, offering businesses an ever-improving, state-of-the-art AI ecosystem.

To summarize, the Dynamics 365 AI ecosystem is a complex yet harmonious orchestration of multiple components—each contributing its unique capabilities but functioning as a coherent whole. This section has provided you with a comprehensive understanding of how data storage, AI models, Cognitive Services, and integration interfaces work in synergy to deliver advanced analytics, machine learning, and intelligent automation. Such an integrated approach ensures that businesses can extract valuable insights to optimize operations effectively. With this knowledge in hand, you're well equipped to grasp the remarkable capabilities and adaptability that Dynamics 365 AI brings to the table.

Integration considerations and best practices

Integration is often the key hurdle to adopting any new technology, and Dynamics 365 AI is no exception. However, its architecture and components are designed with integration in mind, making it possible for organizations to fit it seamlessly into their existing technology stacks. This section aims to provide valuable insights into the practical aspects of integrating Dynamics 365 AI into your existing systems and workflows effectively. The topics include data integration, security measures, scalability, and performance optimization. Each of these areas is critical for maximizing the utility of Dynamics 365 AI and avoiding the common pitfalls that can stifle your AI-driven initiatives.

Data integration – the starting point

Effective data integration is the foundation upon which all AI activities are built. Before diving into machine learning models or advanced analytics, you need to ensure that data flows seamlessly from your existing systems into the Dynamics 365 AI environment. To facilitate this, make use of connectors that link your current databases, ERP systems, or CRM platforms to Azure Data Lake, the primary data storage component in Dynamics 365 AI. These connectors can be pre-built or customized and should be chosen based on your specific needs. Implement batch and real-time data transfer protocols to ensure that the AI models always work with up-to-date information, thereby improving the accuracy of insights and predictions.

Security measures – non-negotiable

Security isn't just a consideration; it's an imperative, especially when integrating a new component such as Dynamics 365 AI into an existing architecture. Use robust authentication mechanisms such as OAuth2 and employ encryption to protect data in transit and at rest. Adhering to GDPR or HIPAA compliance based on your industry is also essential. The platform's inherent security features can be supplemented with additional firewalls, virtual private clouds, or other security measures to protect sensitive data. Remember, a compromised system can nullify all the efficiency gains made through AI.

Scalability – planning for growth

Dynamics 365 AI, being cloud-native, offers excellent scalability options, but it's essential to plan for it proactively. If your data needs are expected to grow exponentially, make sure you allocate sufficient resources in Azure Data Lake and adjust the machine learning models accordingly. Evaluate the pricing tiers for different components to ensure that scaling up doesn't lead to budget overruns. Testing the system under simulated high loads will also give you an understanding of its performance boundaries, helping you make informed decisions about when and how to scale.

Performance optimization – getting the most out of your system

A well-integrated Dynamics 365 AI system should not just be secure and scalable; it should also perform efficiently. Performance optimization involves fine-tuning various settings, from the data ingestion rates in Azure Data Lake to the processing capabilities of machine learning models. Use performance metrics to identify bottlenecks and then adjust configurations or allocate additional resources to resolve them. The tools within Azure can help you monitor performance in real time, enabling timely interventions that keep your system running smoothly.

Documentation and training – the human element

While this is often overlooked, having comprehensive documentation for your integration process can be invaluable. This will serve as a guide for both your current team and any future staff that need to understand the system. Training your team on the nuances of the newly integrated Dynamics 365 AI components is equally essential. Your AI initiatives can only be as effective as the people managing them.

The iterative nature of integration

Lastly, it's crucial to understand that integration is not a one-time task but an ongoing process. As Dynamics 365 AI receives updates and as your organization's needs evolve, continuous adjustments will be required. Adopt an agile approach and keep iterating your integration strategies to align with these changes.

To wrap up, the effective integration of Dynamics 365 AI is multi-faceted, requiring diligent planning and execution across various domains such as data integration, security, scalability, and performance. By understanding and implementing best practices in each of these areas, you're not just ensuring the seamless incorporation of AI into your existing systems; you are also positioning your organization to extract the maximum benefit from your Dynamics 365 AI investment. This section has equipped you with the practical know-how to navigate the complexities of this integration and leverage the full potential that Dynamics 365 AI can bring to your organization.

The journey through the architecture and integration of Microsoft Dynamics 365 AI has been comprehensive, delving deep into the complex yet highly adaptable structure that underpins this powerful suite. Starting from an understanding of its underlying architecture, we traversed through the key components and how they interact, touching upon the critical elements such as data storage, AI models, and cognitive services. These components don't function in isolation; their true power lies in their orchestrated operations, fueling analytics, machine learning, and intelligent automation to generate actionable business insights.

Summary

Data integration has emerged as a linchpin and a foundational step that has to be handled with precision to ensure that the rest of a system functions as intended. Without effective data integration, even the most advanced AI models and analytics engines can fall short. Security measures, too, have been shown to be non-negotiable, affecting not only the trustworthiness of the system but also its compliance with legal and industry-specific requirements.

Next, scalability and performance optimization are twin considerations that can dictate the long-term success of your Dynamics 365 AI implementation. Scalability ensures your system can grow with your business, and performance optimization guarantees that this growth occurs in an efficient, cost-effective manner. These two aspects, if managed well, can provide your business with a competitive edge, ensuring that your technology investment yields maximum returns.

Finally, let's not forget the human element—the staff who will operate and manage this system. Training and comprehensive documentation can make or break the effectiveness of your Dynamics 365 AI components, no matter how well they have been integrated.

In wrapping up, it's important to emphasize the iterative nature of all things related to Dynamics 365 AI. As your business evolves, so too will your needs and the technology itself. Keeping up to date with the latest updates and best practices can go a long way in ensuring that you continue to harness the full power of Dynamics 365 AI.

This chapter has aimed to equip you with a well-rounded understanding and practical guidance to effectively integrate Dynamics 365 AI into your existing systems. You're now prepared to move beyond theory into actionable steps, leveraging the capabilities of Dynamics 365 AI to drive intelligent decision-making and operational excellence in your organization.

Questions

1. What is the importance of data integration in the architecture of Dynamics 365 AI?

2. What role do security measures play in Dynamics 365 AI?

3. Why are scalability and performance optimization crucial for Dynamics 365 AI implementations?

4. What is the significance of human elements such as staff training and documentation in the effective implementation of Dynamics 365 AI?

Answers

1. Data integration is foundational to the effective functioning of Dynamics 365 AI. Without effective data integration, even advanced AI models and analytics engines can fall short of providing accurate and actionable insights. It acts as the linchpin that holds the various components together and ensures seamless operations.

2. Security measures are non-negotiable components of Dynamics 365 AI that affect both the trustworthiness and legal compliance of the system. Implementing robust security protocols ensures the safety of data and the integrity of the AI models, ultimately affecting the overall effectiveness and compliance of the Dynamics 365 AI system.

3. Scalability ensures that the Dynamics 365 AI system can grow alongside the business, adapting to increased data loads and more complex analytical requirements. Performance optimization ensures that this growth occurs in an efficient and cost-effective manner. Together, they can provide a competitive edge and ensure maximum returns on technology investment.

4. The human element can make or break the effectiveness of Dynamics 365 AI. Adequate training and comprehensive documentation are essential for staff who will operate and manage the system. Proper training ensures that the capabilities of Dynamics 365 AI are fully leveraged and that the system functions at its optimal effectiveness.

Part 2: Implementing Dynamics 365 AI Across Business Functions

In this essential part of our book, we focus on how Dynamics 365 AI can be practically applied to improve major areas of business like sales, customer service, marketing, and finance. We aim to demonstrate how strategic utilization of technology can revolutionize and improve the operational efficiency of companies. This part is all about exploring the ways Dynamics 365 AI can make current processes better and open up new possibilities for businesses to innovate and connect with their customers and markets.

This part has the following chapters:

- *Chapter 3, Implementing Dynamics 365 AI for Sales Insights*
- *Chapter 4, Driving Customer Service Excellence with Dynamics 365 AI*
- *Chapter 5, Marketing Optimization with Dynamics 365 AI*
- *Chapter 6, Financial Analytics with Dynamics 365 AI*

Implementing Dynamics 365 AI for Sales Insights

In the vast, constantly evolving landscape of today's business world, **artificial intelligence** (**AI**) has steadfastly anchored itself as a pivotal force driving the future of sales. The fusion of AI with the already potent capabilities of Dynamics 365 sets the stage for a transformative journey—one where data isn't just accumulated but actively speaks, offering profound insights and directions. This chapter beckons readers to delve into that intricate dance between AI's analytical prowess and Dynamics 365's robust suite, elucidating how this combination is redefining the paradigms of sales strategies and practices.

Dynamics 365, when bolstered with AI, emerges not merely as another technical platform but as a seasoned strategist, capable of navigating the labyrinthine intricacies of contemporary sales scenarios. It's a transformative journey we embark upon, beginning with *Leveraging AI for customer segmentation and targeting*. Here, we meticulously dissect how AI parses vast troves of data, discerning patterns and insights, enabling businesses to craft marketing strategies that target the right audience with a laser-like focus. Every segment, every individual becomes an opportunity waiting to be tapped, and AI becomes the compass pointing to these lucrative avenues.

Progressing further, we dive deep into *Predictive lead scoring and opportunity management*, a section where the prescient nature of AI comes to the fore. Amid the overwhelming sea of potential leads, not all are golden opportunities. AI, with its uncanny knack for foresight, sifts through these, prioritizing those that promise maximum yield. But the journey doesn't stop at identification. As we segue into *Personalization and recommendation engines for sales effectiveness*, the narrative shifts to underline the essence of modern commerce. In a world awash with products and services, differentiation lies in delivering personalized experiences. With AI's nuanced understanding of individual preferences, businesses are empowered to craft interactions that are not just transactions but tailored dialogues, echoing the unique needs and aspirations of each customer.

We will cover these topics in the following headings:

- Leveraging AI for customer segmentation and targeting
- Predictive lead scoring and opportunity management
- Personalization and recommendation engines for sales effectiveness
- Examples
- Limitations and pitfalls of using AI for sales

Leveraging AI for customer segmentation and targeting

In today's data-rich digital landscape, the role of AI in revolutionizing customer segmentation and targeting is undeniable. Dynamics 365, combined with advanced AI algorithms, elevates this revolution, bringing forth intricate, data-driven, and actionable insights that empower businesses to interact with their audiences in more personalized and impactful ways.

Segmentation beyond the surface

Historically, customer segmentation was largely demographic. Businesses would categorize their audience based on age, gender, geographic location, and perhaps income. But with the introduction of AI, this has evolved dramatically. Now, companies can not only use demographic data but can also delve deep into psychographic segmentation, categorizing customers based on lifestyles, behaviors, and preferences.

Consider a streaming service platform that previously segmented its audience as "young adults aged 18-25." With AI, this could evolve into "young adults aged 18-25 who prefer indie films, watch late at night, and frequently share content with their network." Such pinpointed segmentation makes the service's recommendations far more precise, enhancing user satisfaction.

Refining targeting strategies

Once businesses have their segments, the next step is to tailor their messages and services to each segment. This process, known as **targeting**, has been fundamentally changed by AI. Dynamics 365 AI can analyze vast amounts of data to derive not just who a company should target but how and when.

For instance, an online fashion retailer might traditionally target "women aged 30-40." However, with AI's granularity, they could target "women aged 30-40 who have recently viewed sportswear, interacted with fitness influencers on social media, and shop frequently on weekend mornings." Such specific targeting can then guide personalized email campaigns, web advertisements, or even the timing of flash sales.

Predictive analysis – the game-changer

Beyond immediate targeting, AI's capability for predictive analysis is groundbreaking. It doesn't just use existing data to draw insights but forecasts potential future trends. Imagine a health food brand discovering, through AI analysis, that there's a burgeoning interest in a particular superfood. They could capitalize on this emerging trend, launching new products or campaigns before the competition catches on.

Dynamics 365 – a bedrock of quality data

Integral to the effectiveness of AI in segmentation and targeting is the quality and breadth of data it's fed. This is where Dynamics 365 shines. It captures a plethora of data points, from customer interactions, transactions, feedback, and more. When this rich data reservoir is harnessed by sophisticated AI algorithms, the result is a symphony of insights that are not just accurate but actionable.

Real-world impact – a clothing brand case study

To truly understand the implications, let's consider a practical example. A global clothing brand, leveraging Dynamics 365 AI, realized a trend among *young professionals in urban areas* showing increasing interest in sustainable fashion. Instead of launching a broad-based sustainable line, they segmented further: creating collections for *young female professionals who favor minimalist designs* and *young male professionals who lean toward bold patterns*. The result? Two distinct, AI-driven lines that resonated deeply with their target segments, leading to increased sales and brand loyalty.

In conclusion, the modern business world isn't about casting the widest net but about ensuring that the net is cast in the most fruitful waters. AI, especially when integrated with platforms such as Dynamics 365, equips businesses with the intelligence and tools to do just that. Through nuanced segmentation and predictive targeting, companies can deliver products, services, and messages that resonate, fostering deeper connections and driving business growth.

Predictive lead scoring and opportunity management

In today's age of digital commerce, where businesses are continuously overwhelmed with a plethora of leads, discerning the diamonds in the rough becomes paramount. Dynamics 365 AI's predictive lead scoring system emerges as a beacon, illuminating the path toward the most promising leads with the highest conversion potential.

Anatomy of predictive lead scoring in Dynamics 365 AI

Dynamics 365 AI's predictive lead scoring is not simply an upgraded feature but a holistic tool embedded deeply within its system. At its core lies cutting-edge **machine learning** (**ML**) algorithms that meticulously examine historical sales data, engagement patterns, and more to attribute scores to new leads. But the intelligence doesn't end there; as the flow of data continues, these algorithms self-adjust and evolve, resulting in ever-improving accuracy and relevance of lead scores.

Consider the journey of John, a hypothetical lead. Traditional lead scoring might award him points for being a CEO or living in a metropolitan area. However, Dynamics 365 AI digs deeper: it considers John's interactions with marketing emails, his browsing patterns on the business website, and even the frequency and duration of his visits. If he repeatedly examines a product's technical specifications or watches product demos, the system recognizes his deeper interest and scores him accordingly.

The transformative nature of predictive scoring in sales

For sales teams, predictive scoring is a game-changer. With leads being constantly evaluated and ranked, sales representatives are no longer shooting in the dark. Instead, they receive a prioritized list of leads, enabling them to dedicate their efforts where they count most.

For instance, Sarah, a sales representative, no longer wastes her time on leads that only give a fleeting glance at the website. Instead, Dynamics 365 AI directs her to engage with leads who've shown tangible interest, such as those who've downloaded whitepapers or attended webinars. This targeted approach not only increases her conversion rate but also boosts her morale.

Holistic opportunity management with Dynamics 365 AI

But the power of Dynamics 365 AI doesn't just lie in grading leads. It offers a comprehensive suite for opportunity management. Based on a lead's interactions, the AI suggests tailored strategies for engagement. If, for instance, a potential lead lingers on a page about cloud solutions but doesn't make a purchase, the AI might propose offering them an exclusive webinar on cloud integration or a limited-time discount.

Moreover, for leads that have cooled off or lost engagement, Dynamics 365 AI isn't quick to write them off. It recommends re-engagement strategies, whether it's a sneak peek at an upcoming product or a personalized touchpoint through a sales representative.

Deep dive into predictive analysis and its implications

One of the standout features of Dynamics 365 AI is its predictive analytical capability. By assimilating data from diverse sources and recognizing intricate patterns, the AI forecasts upcoming market changes or emerging preferences. A company could, for instance, identify a budding trend in eco-conscious products before they become mainstream, allowing them to pivot their product line and marketing strategies proactively.

An illustration of predictive lead scoring

Consider Bella's Boutique, an e-commerce platform selling artisanal products. With Dynamics 365 AI, Bella notices a trend: leads that engage with "handmade" tags on products often tend to finalize purchases when introduced to creator stories. Acting on this, she introduces a new marketing strategy, sending personalized emails to such leads with heartwarming stories of the artisans. This small change leads to a notable uptick in sales. Concurrently, Bella also detects a growing interest in sustainable packaging. By switching to eco-friendly packaging and highlighting it, she's not only meeting a demand but setting a trend, putting her ahead of competitors.

In essence, Dynamics 365 AI's predictive lead scoring and robust opportunity management not only optimize the present but also anticipate the future, granting businesses the twin powers of foresight and agility. The end result? Enhanced sales strategies, more effective engagements, and a streamlined path to sustained business growth.

Personalization and recommendation engines for sales effectiveness

The paradigm of modern sales has shifted drastically from volume-based approaches to value-driven interactions. Dynamics 365 AI is at the forefront of this transition, embedding personalization into the DNA of sales strategies. The current market dynamics, dominated by discerning consumers and clients, demand tailored experiences. These personalized interactions, fostered by Dynamics 365 AI's capabilities, can significantly enhance user engagement, improve conversion rates, and solidify brand loyalty.

An example of a real-world implementation of a value-based approach could be a boutique cosmetic brand that faces challenges in a market dominated by larger competitors. The brand realizes that the key to standing out is not just increasing sales volume but creating value-driven, personalized experiences for its customers. The brand can implement Dynamics 365 AI to analyze customer data, such as past purchases, browsing behaviors, and customer feedback. It can use the data to understand individual customer preferences and needs. For instance, it can analyze past purchases to recommend products that complement that customer's existing skincare routine. It can also suggest products based on the customer's skin type, concerns, and perhaps even interactive quizzes. This approach leads to an increase in user engagement as customers appreciate the curated recommendations that mirror an in-store consultation experience with a professional. The brand becomes a trusted advisor, not just a retailer. AI has helped the cosmetic brand transition from a volume-based approach to a value-driven strategy with improved user engagement, conversion rates, and building brand loyalty.

Data-driven personalization in Dynamics 365 AI

At the core of Dynamics 365 AI's personalization engine lies a potent combination of data analytics and ML. By capturing and analyzing multifaceted customer data—encompassing purchase histories, interaction metrics, and even sentiment analysis from reviews—the platform gleans deep insights into individual user personas. This intricate understanding allows the system to predict what a user might be interested in next, offering a timely and relevant sales pitch or product suggestion.

Take the hypothetical scenario of a company, CyberSafe, that offers digital security solutions. Their sales team notices that Ms. Thompson, an executive from a growing start-up, often browses their enterprise-level cybersecurity offerings. Using Dynamics 365 AI, they not only track her visits but also analyze her queries and interactions. By merging these insights, they can draft a proposal addressing her company's specific challenges, increasing the likelihood of a successful deal.

Recommendation engines – beyond the obvious

Dynamics 365 AI doesn't just stop at personalization; its recommendation engines take sales strategies several notches higher. These engines harness algorithms that process user behaviors, past purchases, and more to offer intuitive product or service suggestions, often unveiling needs the client hadn't even recognized.

Consider TechBlitz, a fictional IT services company. By utilizing Dynamics 365 AI, they discern that businesses that adopt their cloud services often look for cybersecurity solutions within the next quarter. Leveraging this insight, TechBlitz can bundle or offer special deals combining these services, positioning themselves as a comprehensive solutions provider.

Feedback loops and iterative refinement

No AI system, no matter how advanced, can be entirely foolproof from the outset. Recognizing this, Dynamics 365 AI integrates adaptive feedback mechanisms. These mechanisms gauge user reactions to recommendations—whether they embraced, ignored, or rejected them. Such feedback is invaluable. It helps refine the underlying algorithms, ensuring their output remains aligned with evolving customer preferences and market trends.

In the real world, a home décor retailer specializing in custom furniture and home accessories leveraged Dynamics 365 AI to enhance its product recommendation system using feedback loops and iterative refinement. After the initial deployment, the retailer noticed that not all recommendations based on customer browsing history and past purchases were hitting the mark. Some customers were not engaging with the suggested items. To address this, the retailer integrated Dynamics 365 AI's adaptive feedback mechanisms that tracked how customers interacted with the recommendations. They noted which items were added to the cart, ignored, and rejected. The feedback became crucial to refining the AI recommendation algorithms. For instance, if a significant number of customers ignored recommendations for modern-style lamps, the AI would adjust its algorithm to either change the style of the products or target a different customer that may be more interested in modern décor.

Over time, the adaptive feedback led to a noticeable improvement in recommendation relevance and an increase in customer engagement and purchasing of recommended products. Adaptive feedback allowed the home décor retailer to offer more accurate and appealing recommendations, enhance customer satisfaction, and boost sales.

Personalization in action – a real-world glimpse

In the dynamic realm of e-commerce, personalization can be the defining factor between fleeting transactions and sustained customer relationships. Picture EcoWear, a sustainable fashion brand. Using Dynamics 365 AI, they tailor their online shopping experience for every user. When Ms. Green, a returning customer, logs in, she's greeted with suggestions based on her past purchases, browsing behavior, and even her feedback on previous products.

Suppose she had earlier shown interest in sustainable footwear. The next time she visits, she might find recommendations for a new line of eco-friendly shoes or care products to extend the lifespan of her purchases. Such attentive touches transform her shopping experience, making it more intuitive and enjoyable.

Dynamics 365 AI's prowess in personalization and recommendation is a testament to the evolving nature of sales. It's no longer about casting a wide net and hoping for the best. It's about understanding each customer, predicting their needs, and offering value at every touchpoint. Through its advanced algorithms and data-driven insights, Dynamics 365 AI equips businesses to navigate this new sales frontier, fostering deeper customer relationships and consistently driving sales performance.

Examples

Let's consider use cases that reflect challenges companies face in the real world and how they can leverage Dynamics 365 AI to solve problems and improve their processes.

Example 1 – ElevateApparel's customer segmentation triumph

The challenge

ElevateApparel, an up-and-coming online fashion brand, wanted to launch its summer collection. They aimed to not only entice their existing customer base but also attract new customers. However, with an ever-growing database, manually segmenting and targeting customers based on changing preferences was daunting.

Implementation of Dynamics 365 AI

ElevateApparel employed Dynamics 365 AI's customer segmentation tool to dissect their database. The AI system analyzed customers' purchase histories, online interactions, and even returned items. It discovered patterns such as a surge in pastel color purchases during spring or a specific age group leaning toward boho-chic.

Using this insight, ElevateApparel launched tailored marketing campaigns. For instance, college students received ads showcasing affordable, trendy pieces, while working professionals got a glimpse of the brand's premium line.

The outcome

The campaign was a smashing success. ElevateApparel witnessed a 50% uptick in sales compared to their previous collection launches, and the brand received significant acclaim for its *intuitively curated* fashion lines.

Example 2 – ProTech Solutions and the predictive power

The challenge

ProTech Solutions, a B2B tech service provider, had a vast lead database but a low conversion rate. The sales team was overwhelmed, unable to differentiate between cold leads and potential gold mines.

Implementation of Dynamics 365 AI

ProTech harnessed Dynamics 365 AI for predictive lead scoring. The system began ranking leads based on various metrics—past interactions, company size, the potential need for ProTech's services, and even recent tech acquisitions.

With these scores in hand, the sales team could prioritize their efforts. High-ranking leads were immediately addressed with personalized pitches and demos, while lower-scoring ones were nurtured through informative webinars and newsletters.

The outcome

ProTech's conversion rates skyrocketed. They achieved a 40% increase in new contracts within a quarter. The sales team, now more focused and less stressed, credited their newfound success to the AI's predictive insights.

Example 3 – NovelReads' personalized book journey

The challenge

NovelReads, an e-book platform, faced declining user engagement. While they had a vast collection, readers often felt lost and unsure of what to read next, leading to reduced session times and infrequent visits.

Implementation of Dynamics 365 AI

NovelReads integrated Dynamics 365 AI's recommendation engine. By analyzing reading patterns, genres preferred, and reader reviews, the platform began suggesting tailored reading lists to its users. Historical romance lovers got recommendations of not just top-rated books but also hidden gems. Mystery lovers were directed toward new releases and classic whodunits.

To enhance sales effectiveness, special bundles were crafted based on AI insights. For example, fantasy lovers received bundled offers of trilogies or entire series at discounted rates.

The outcome

NovelReads experienced a revival. Session times doubled, sales increased by 35%, and users started actively reviewing and rating more books, further enhancing the AI's recommendation capabilities. The platform transformed from a simple e-bookstore to a reader's paradise, curating unique reading journeys for each user.

Limitations and pitfalls of using AI for sales

Using AI for sales clearly provides numerous benefits. However, implementing AI can also pose challenges. AI systems rely heavily on data from training and operations. The accuracy and effectiveness of AI in sales are directly proportional to the quality and quantity of data available. Poor, biased, or incomplete data can lead to inaccurate predictions and recommendations, potentially harming sales efforts. An over-reliance on AI can also lead to a reduction in personal interactions between sales representatives and customers. This might be detrimental in scenarios where AI can't quite replace human judgment, which is critical for closing sales and building customer sales relationships. One benefit of AI is that it is rapidly evolving, but that can also be a downside. Evolving technology requires continuous updates, improvements, and keeping up with the latest developments. This can be resource-intensive, and there is a risk of technologies becoming obsolete quickly. While AI in sales presents significant opportunities for efficiency and growth, these potential drawbacks need to be carefully managed. Balancing AI-driven strategies with human insights and ethical considerations is key to harnessing the full benefits of AI in sales.

Summary

The digital transformation that businesses are undergoing in today's era is no longer just about transitioning operations online; it's about intelligently leveraging the vast pools of data at our disposal to create more meaningful and efficient interactions with customers. As explored in this chapter, Dynamics 365 AI has proven itself as an invaluable tool for transforming sales operations across diverse industries. From granular customer segmentation to astute lead scoring, and from personalized product recommendations to optimized sales strategies, the capabilities of this platform offer businesses a new paradigm in sales effectiveness.

The examples and use cases emphasized how, when rightly employed, AI-driven insights can directly impact a company's bottom line. ElevateApparel's success in crafting targeted marketing campaigns, ProTech Solutions' breakthrough in lead conversion rates, and NovelReads' achievement in driving user engagement are not isolated stories. They represent the larger narrative of businesses globally reaping the rewards of AI-integrated sales processes. These success tales beckon other organizations to follow suit and reimagine their sales strategies with the intelligence and precision that Dynamics 365 AI offers.

Moreover, the evolution in customer expectations has made it clear: generic interactions no longer cut it. The modern customer expects personalization, precision, and a genuine understanding of their needs. Meeting such demands without an AI-backed system would be a herculean task, if not impossible.

To close, while technology and AI can provide tools and pathways, the true strength lies in how businesses employ these resources to understand and serve their customers better. After all, sales, in its essence, is a dance between human needs and solutions. With Dynamics 365 AI, businesses are more equipped than ever to lead this dance with grace, foresight, and effectiveness. As we venture into further chapters and delve deeper into other Dynamics 365 AI applications, let's carry forward the understanding of how pivotal AI is in setting businesses up for success in the contemporary digital age. For example, in the next chapter, we will explore Dynamics 365 AI's ability to redefine customer service for today's businesses.

Questions

1. In the context of leveraging AI for customer segmentation, what specific data did ElevateApparel analyze using Dynamics 365 AI to create more effective marketing campaigns?

2. How did ProTech Solutions use Dynamics 365 AI's predictive lead scoring to improve their sales team's efficiency?

3. Describe how NovelReads enhanced sales effectiveness using Dynamics 365 AI's recommendation engine.

4. What common challenges can Dynamics 365 AI address in the sales domain, as evidenced by the examples provided in the chapter?

Answers

1. ElevateApparel analyzed customers' purchase histories, online interactions, and returned items to understand preferences and trends, such as a preference for pastel colors during spring or a specific age group's inclination toward boho-chic styles.

2. ProTech Solutions employed Dynamics 365 AI for predictive lead scoring, which ranked leads based on various metrics such as past interactions, company size, the potential need for ProTech's services, and recent tech acquisitions. This allowed the sales team to prioritize high-ranking leads with personalized pitches and demos while nurturing lower-scoring ones differently.

3. NovelReads used Dynamics 365 AI's recommendation engine to analyze reading patterns, preferred genres, and reader reviews to suggest tailored reading lists to its users. To boost sales, they crafted special bundles based on AI insights, such as offering fantasy series at discounted rates.

4. Dynamics 365 AI can tackle challenges such as vast and unsegmented customer databases, low lead conversion rates due to inefficient lead prioritization, and declining user engagement due to a lack of personalized experiences. The examples showcased how businesses can employ AI to dissect databases, prioritize leads, and provide tailored recommendations to enhance sales and engagement.

4

Driving Customer Service Excellence with Dynamics 365 AI

In this chapter, we embark on a comprehensive exploration of Dynamics 365 AI's capabilities in redefining customer service in modern business operations. It delves deeply into how AI integration is enhancing the efficiency and effectiveness of customer interactions, a crucial aspect of maintaining competitive edge and customer loyalty in today's market.

The chapter commences with a detailed look into *Enhancing customer experience with virtual agents and chatbots*. This section is dedicated to understanding how Dynamics 365 AI deploys these advanced tools to handle various customer service tasks. It examines the sophisticated algorithms that enable virtual agents and chatbots to provide instant, accurate responses and manage high-volume customer inquiries. The focus here is not just on the functionality of these AI-driven tools but also on their design and deployment strategies, user experience, and the overall impact on customer satisfaction and engagement.

We then progress to a vital component of modern customer service technology—*AI-powered sentiment analysis and customer sentiment tracking*. This part of the chapter provides an in-depth analysis of how Dynamics 365 AI uses **natural language processing** (**NLP**) and **machine learning** (**ML**) to interpret and respond to the emotional tone of customer communications. By analyzing nuances in customer feedback, complaints, and inquiries, the system offers valuable insights into the customer experience, allowing businesses to adapt and personalize their services in a more informed and responsive manner.

Following this, the chapter addresses *Intelligent routing and case management for efficient support*. Here, we dissect the capabilities of Dynamics 365 AI in managing and directing customer inquiries to the most suitable service channels and representatives. This section delves into the AI's decision-making processes, detailing how it assesses the nature of customer issues and streamlines the workflow to enhance the overall efficiency of the customer service team.

The final part of the chapter, *Real-world examples of AI-driven customer service enhancements*, brings the theoretical and technical aspects into a real-world context. It presents a series of case studies illustrating how various organizations have integrated Dynamics 365 AI into their customer service processes. These success stories are dissected to reveal not only the outcomes but also the challenges and strategies involved in implementing AI-driven customer service solutions. These narratives provide a practical perspective, showcasing the transformative impact of AI on customer service efficiency, problem resolution, and **customer relationship management (CRM)**.

Specifically, we will cover the following main topics:

- Enhancing customer experience with virtual agents and chatbots
- AI-powered sentiment analysis and customer sentiment tracking
- Intelligent routing and case management for efficient support
- Real-world examples of AI-driven customer service enhancements

Throughout this chapter, readers will gain not only a thorough understanding of the functionalities and advantages of Dynamics 365 AI in customer service but also insights into implementation tactics, challenges, and best practices. The chapter aims to equip professionals and decision-makers with the knowledge and tools needed to harness AI's potential in enhancing customer service, thereby driving improved customer satisfaction, loyalty, and ultimately, business success in the digital era.

Enhancing customer experience with virtual agents and chatbots

A defining feature of modern virtual agents and chatbots is their ability for continuous learning and adaptation, powered by advanced ML algorithms. This attribute ensures that they not only respond to customer inquiries but also evolve from each interaction, becoming more nuanced and effective over time. Next, we will address key aspects of virtual agents and chatbots, including the mechanics of continuous learning, feedback loops and data analysis, training, real-time performance adjustments, and integration of human feedback.

The mechanics of continuous learning

Virtual agents and chatbots are built on ML models that thrive on data. Each customer interaction is an opportunity for these models to learn and improve. For instance, when a chatbot successfully resolves a customer's query, this outcome feeds back into the system, teaching the model about effective responses. Conversely, if a query is escalated to a human agent, the model analyzes what went wrong and adjusts its algorithms accordingly.

Feedback loops and data analysis

A key aspect of this learning process is the feedback loop. Data from customer interactions, whether it's the text of a conversation, the chosen responses, or the time taken to resolve issues, is continually fed back into the system. This ongoing process allows AI models to analyze patterns, identify areas of improvement, and refine their understanding of customer needs and language nuances.

Example of adaptation in action

Consider a virtual agent initially programmed to handle basic queries about product features. Over time, as it encounters a wider variety of questions, it starts to recognize and understand more complex inquiries, such as those relating to product compatibility or troubleshooting. For instance, if a new software update leads to common issues, the chatbot quickly learns from the influx of related queries, adapting its knowledge base to provide more efficient responses to these new, frequently asked questions.

Training with synthetic data

Another aspect of continuous learning involves training the AI models with synthetic data-simulated scenarios that enhance the chatbot's ability to handle a wide range of potential conversations. This proactive learning ensures the chatbot is not solely reliant on past interactions and is prepared for less common queries.

Real-time performance adjustments

Chatbots and virtual agents also employ real-time performance adjustments. If a chatbot detects confusion or dissatisfaction in a customer's response, such as repeated questions or the use of negative language, it can immediately adjust its approach or escalate the issue to a human agent.

Evolving with consumer trends

The ability of virtual agents to adapt goes beyond individual interactions. They also evolve with changing consumer trends and preferences. AI algorithms can detect shifts in customer behavior or new patterns in inquiries, allowing the chatbot to stay relevant and up to date with market dynamics.

Integration with human feedback

Incorporating human feedback into the learning loop is crucial. Periodic reviews by human agents and incorporating their insights into the AI model help in refining the chatbot's responses, ensuring they align with the business's communication standards and customer service goals.

The continuous learning and adaptation capabilities of virtual agents and chatbots signify a monumental shift in automated customer service technology. By evolving from each interaction and staying attuned to the latest trends and data insights, these AI-driven tools are not just answering customer queries but are constantly enhancing the quality and relevance of their interactions. This dynamic learning process is central to providing a customer service experience that is not only efficient but also deeply attuned to the evolving needs and expectations of customers.

AI-powered sentiment analysis and customer sentiment tracking

In the landscape of AI-enhanced customer service, sentiment analysis and customer sentiment tracking stand out as pivotal tools. These AI-driven capabilities extend the function of virtual agents and chatbots beyond mere transactional interactions, allowing them to gauge and respond to emotional undertones in customer communications. This section explores the technical aspects, applications, and impacts of sentiment analysis in modern customer service.

Technical aspects of sentiment analysis

Sentiment analysis in AI systems primarily relies on NLP and ML. NLP interprets and understands human language, enabling the AI to process not only what is being said but also how it's being said. By analyzing word choice, sentence structure, and even the rhythm of the customer's language, the AI can identify whether the sentiment is positive, negative, or neutral.

ML for enhanced sentiment detection

ML models in sentiment analysis are trained on vast datasets containing various customer interactions, encompassing text from chat logs, emails, social media posts, and more. These models learn to recognize patterns associated with different emotional states. For instance, repeated use of words such as "disappointed" or "frustrated" might signal dissatisfaction, prompting a different response strategy from the AI.

Real-time sentiment tracking and response adaptation

One of the most significant applications of sentiment analysis is in real-time response adaptation. If a chatbot detects negative sentiment in a customer's message, it can adjust its responses to be more empathetic or escalate the issue to a human agent. For example, if a customer expresses frustration over a product issue, the chatbot might respond with language that acknowledges the inconvenience and offers immediate assistance or compensation.

Predictive analytics in sentiment analysis

Predictive analytics in sentiment analysis involve using historical data to anticipate future customer emotions and reactions. This can be particularly useful in predicting potential issues with products or services before they become widespread problems, allowing businesses to proactively address them.

Sentiment analysis for personalized marketing

Beyond customer service, sentiment analysis can be leveraged for personalized marketing efforts. By understanding the prevailing sentiments of a customer segment, businesses can tailor their marketing strategies, ensuring that the tone and content of their campaigns resonate well with their audience.

Data-driven strategy adjustments

Sentiment analysis provides valuable insights for broader strategic decision-making. Regular sentiment tracking can highlight long-term trends in customer satisfaction and perception, guiding businesses in product development, service improvements, and overall customer experience strategy.

Challenges and ethical and security considerations

While sentiment analysis offers immense benefits, it also presents challenges. Ethical considerations around privacy and data handling must be rigorously managed. Organizations must implement robust data protection measures, such as encryption in transit and at rest, to secure this data against unauthorized access. Additionally, adhering to privacy laws and regulations, such as the **General Data Protection Regulation** (**GDPR**) in Europe or the **California Consumer Privacy Act** (**CCPA**) in California is essential to protect customer rights and maintain trust.

When analyzing customer sentiment, it's often unnecessary to link analysis back to individual identities. Anonymizing or pseudonymizing data helps mitigate privacy risks. Data masking techniques can also be used, especially in development and testing environments, to protect sensitive information while maintaining the utility of the data for analysis purposes.

In addition, keeping detailed logs and continuously monitoring access and usage of sentiment analysis tools are vital for security. Audit trails can help track who accessed what data and when, providing an essential tool for identifying and investigating suspicious activities that could indicate a security breach. Implementing stringent access controls ensures that only authorized personnel have access to sentiment analysis tools and the data they process. **Role-based access control** (**RBAC**) and the **principle of least privilege** (**PoLP**) can minimize the risk of data breaches by limiting access based on users' roles and their need to access specific data for their job functions.

The dynamic nature of threats necessitates regular security assessments of AI-powered sentiment analysis systems. Vulnerability scanning, penetration testing, and reviewing AI models for potential biases or flaws can help identify and mitigate security risks proactively.

By incorporating these security and ethical considerations, organizations can not only leverage Dynamics 365 AI to enhance customer service through sentiment analysis but also ensure that they do so in a secure, privacy-respecting manner. This dual focus on innovation and security is essential for maintaining customer trust and achieving service excellence in today's digital landscape.

Intelligent routing and case management for efficient support

In the realm of customer service, the efficiency and effectiveness of support systems are paramount. With the advent of AI technology, intelligent routing and case management have emerged as key features, significantly enhancing the quality of customer support. This section delves into the mechanics, applications, and impact of these AI-driven systems in modern customer service environments.

The mechanics of intelligent routing

Intelligent routing in AI-driven systems involves the automated distribution of customer inquiries to the most appropriate service agent or department. This process is based on a variety of factors, including the nature of the inquiry, the customer's history, and the expertise of available agents. AI algorithms analyze incoming requests in real time, quickly determining the best course of action, whether it's routing to a human agent, a chatbot with specific expertise, or even escalating to higher-level support.

Enhanced efficiency with AI algorithms

AI algorithms play a crucial role in optimizing the routing process. They continuously learn from past interactions, improving their ability to categorize and direct inquiries effectively. For example, an AI system might recognize that technical questions about a certain product are best handled by a specific team, while billing queries are more efficiently resolved by another.

Case management and automated resolution

Beyond routing, AI systems also assist in case management. They can track the status of open cases, send follow-up reminders, and even suggest solutions based on previous similar cases. In some instances, AI can automate resolutions for common issues, closing cases quickly and efficiently without the need for human intervention.

Predictive analysis in case prioritization

Predictive analysis plays a pivotal role in case management. AI systems can prioritize cases based on urgency, customer value, or likelihood of escalation. This predictive capability ensures that critical issues are addressed promptly, improving overall customer satisfaction and reducing the risk of escalated complaints.

Integration with CRM systems

The integration of AI-driven routing and case management with CRM systems enhances the overall customer service framework. This integration ensures a seamless flow of customer data across the system, enabling personalized and contextually aware support.

Real-time adjustments for peak efficiency

AI systems in customer service are designed for real-time adjustments. They can adapt to changing scenarios, such as sudden spikes in inquiry volume or shifts in the nature of queries, ensuring that the support system remains efficient under varying conditions.

Challenges in implementation

Implementing intelligent routing and case management systems is not without challenges. It requires a careful balance between AI automation and human oversight to ensure that customer interactions remain personal and empathetic. Additionally, training AI systems to understand the nuances of different types of inquiries can be a complex process.

Intelligent routing and case management through AI significantly streamline customer support operations. By ensuring that inquiries are directed to the most suitable agents and managed effectively, these systems not only enhance the efficiency of the support process but also greatly improve the customer experience. As businesses continue to navigate the challenges of customer service in a digital age, AI-driven routing and case management stand out as essential tools for delivering high-quality, efficient customer support.

Real-world examples of AI-driven customer service enhancements

One way to explore how to leverage AI-driven customer service is to consider real-world uses. How can we implement virtual agents and chatbots to provide efficient and acceptable customer service? Next are several examples.

Example 1 – Global bank incorporates AI for efficient customer query handling

The challenge: A major global bank was facing challenges with managing the high volume of customer service inquiries they received daily. The bank struggled with long wait times and misrouted queries, leading to customer dissatisfaction and increased operational costs.

The AI solution: The bank implemented an AI-driven customer service system with intelligent routing capabilities. The AI system was designed to analyze incoming queries in real time, categorizing them based on complexity and customer history, and then directing them to the appropriate support channel, whether it was a chatbot for simpler queries or human agents for more complex issues.

The outcome: The adoption of AI-driven routing led to a significant reduction in response times and a more efficient allocation of customer service resources. Customer satisfaction scores improved due to faster resolution times, and the bank also saw a reduction in operational costs as the AI system helped optimize staff workload and reduce the need for extra human agent intervention.

Example 2 – E-commerce platform utilizes AI for personalized customer support

The challenge: An expanding e-commerce platform was struggling to provide personalized support to its growing customer base. With a diverse range of products and customer inquiries, the company found it challenging to maintain a high level of customer service quality.

The AI solution: The company integrated AI-powered chatbots capable of sentiment analysis and personalized interactions. These chatbots were connected to the company's CRM system, enabling them to access customer purchase history and preferences, thereby providing more tailored assistance.

The outcome: The introduction of AI-powered chatbots led to an enhanced customer service experience. Customers received personalized product recommendations and quicker solutions to their inquiries. The e-commerce platform experienced an increase in customer engagement, repeat purchases, and overall customer loyalty as a result of the more personalized and efficient support.

Example 3 – Telecom giant implements AI for streamlined case management

The challenge: A leading telecommunications company was experiencing inefficiencies in handling customer service cases. With a vast array of services and customer issues, the company found it challenging to manage and prioritize the high volume of cases efficiently.

The AI solution: The company implemented an AI-based system for intelligent case management. The AI system was designed to prioritize cases based on urgency and customer importance. It also suggested solutions based on similar past cases and could automate responses for common issues.

The outcome: The telecom company saw a significant improvement in case resolution times. The AI system's ability to prioritize and suggest solutions led to quicker resolution of high-priority cases and reduced the burden on customer service agents. As a result, the company reported higher customer satisfaction levels and a noticeable improvement in operational efficiency.

These are only a few of the many types of businesses that can benefit from implementing AI for customer service. AI can improve the handling and prioritization of customer inquiries, leading to better experiences for customers and employees.

Summary

In wrapping up this chapter, *Driving Customer Service Excellence with Dynamics 365 AI*, it's evident that AI's role in customer service goes beyond mere technological enhancement. We've seen how AI-powered tools such as virtual agents, chatbots, and sentiment analysis are fundamentally changing customer support. These tools have streamlined interaction management, providing quick and accurate responses that boost customer satisfaction.

The use of sentiment analysis has been particularly transformative, offering deep insights into customer emotions and enabling more personalized service. Intelligent routing and case management systems have further streamlined customer service processes, ensuring efficient and organized handling of inquiries. Real-world applications across various industries have highlighted the tangible benefits of Dynamics 365 AI, showcasing improvements in efficiency, customer satisfaction, and overall service quality.

As we conclude, Dynamics 365 AI emerges as a crucial element in modern customer service, setting new standards in personalized and effective customer support. Its continued evolution will undoubtedly shape the future of customer service in the digital age, making it essential for businesses aiming for excellence in customer relations.

In the next chapter, we move on to address how AI can optimize marketing efforts and create targeted, meaningful marketing campaigns.

Questions

1. How did the implementation of AI-driven customer service tools impact the global bank mentioned in one of the case studies?

2. How have AI-powered virtual agents and chatbots specifically improved customer service in businesses?

3. What role does sentiment analysis play in AI-enhanced customer service?

4. What was the outcome of the e-commerce platform's integration of AI-powered chatbots for personalized customer support, as described in one of the case studies?

5. How does intelligent routing and case management contribute to the effectiveness of customer service?

Answers

1. In the case study of the global bank, the implementation of AI-driven customer service tools, particularly intelligent routing, significantly improved operational efficiency and customer satisfaction. The AI system efficiently categorized and directed customer inquiries to appropriate support channels, reducing response times and optimizing the workload of customer service staff. This led to a noticeable reduction in operational costs and enhanced the overall customer experience.

2. AI-powered virtual agents and chatbots have enhanced customer service by automating responses and efficiently managing a high volume of customer interactions. This automation allows for quick and accurate support, leading to higher customer satisfaction levels.

3. Sentiment analysis in AI-enhanced customer service helps in understanding and responding to the emotional tones in customer communications. It analyzes customer sentiments in real time, providing deeper insights into customer needs and enabling more personalized and effective service responses.

4. The e-commerce platform's integration of AI-powered chatbots for personalized customer support resulted in increased customer engagement, repeat purchases, and overall customer loyalty. The chatbots, equipped with sentiment analysis and access to customer purchase history, provided tailored assistance and product recommendations. This personalization led to a more engaging shopping experience for customers, contributing to the platform's growth in customer engagement and loyalty.

5. Intelligent routing and case management streamline the process of handling customer inquiries. They ensure that customer issues are directed to the right channels and resolved quickly, increasing operational efficiency and ensuring a more organized approach to customer service.

5
Marketing Optimization with Dynamics 365 AI

In the advancing field of digital marketing, the integration of **artificial intelligence** (**AI**) through platforms such as Microsoft Dynamics 365 is creating a significant shift in marketing strategies. In this chapter, we delve into the transformative impact of AI in the realm of marketing, highlighting how this technology is reshaping marketing efforts to be more effective and data-driven.

We commence our exploration with *AI-driven customer segmentation and campaign targeting*. This section will explore how Dynamics 365 AI utilizes advanced algorithms to analyze extensive customer data. By doing so, it segments customers beyond traditional demographics, considering their behaviors and preferences. This approach allows for highly targeted and efficient marketing campaigns, tailored to meet the specific needs and interests of different customer groups.

Progressing further, the chapter discusses *personalized recommendations and cross-selling opportunities*. Here, the emphasis is on how Dynamics 365 AI can leverage customer interaction data to suggest personalized product recommendations. This capability is crucial for identifying potential sales opportunities, enhancing customer experiences, and increasing the effectiveness of cross-selling strategies.

A key component of modern marketing is the strategic use of social media. Therefore, we dedicate a significant section to *social media sentiment analysis and brand perception insights*. Dynamics 365 AI's ability to analyze social media data is crucial for understanding how a brand is perceived in the public domain. This section will examine how AI tools can parse social media trends, hashtags, and sentiments, providing businesses with essential insights for informed decision-making in marketing and brand management.

The chapter concludes with *Real-world examples and best practices in marketing insights*. This section will present various case studies demonstrating how different companies have successfully integrated Dynamics 365 AI into their marketing strategies. These real-world examples will serve as practical illustrations of AI's capabilities in marketing, offering insights into effective implementation and best practices.

Overall, this chapter aims to provide a comprehensive and detailed guide on utilizing Dynamics 365 AI for marketing optimization. From deep customer insights to advanced engagement strategies, the chapter will highlight how AI is setting new standards in digital marketing, enabling businesses to achieve greater success in their marketing endeavors. As we delve into each topic, readers will gain a clearer understanding of the powerful impact of AI in marketing, opening new opportunities for innovation and growth in the digital marketplace.

Here is a list of the topics covered in this chapter:

- AI-driven customer segmentation and campaign targeting
- Personalized recommendations and cross-selling opportunities
- Social media sentiment analysis and brand perception insights
- Real-world examples and best practices in marketing insights

AI-driven customer segmentation and campaign targeting

In the sphere of modern marketing, Dynamics 365 AI has been a game-changer, particularly in the realm of customer segmentation and campaign targeting. This section delves into the nuanced functionalities of Dynamics 365 AI, showcasing how it's transforming the landscape of targeted marketing with its advanced AI capabilities.

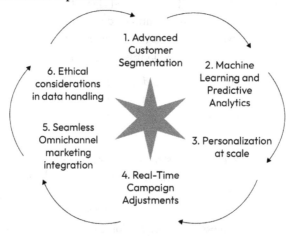

Figure 5.1 – Overview of customer segmentation and campaign targeting

Advanced customer segmentation

Dynamics 365 AI revolutionizes traditional customer segmentation by leveraging **deep machine learning** (DML) algorithms. These algorithms go beyond basic demographics and sift through complex datasets including purchase patterns, interaction histories, and social media engagement. This level of analysis allows Dynamics 365 AI to identify intricate customer segments based on a variety of behavioral and psychographic factors.

For instance, a business using Dynamics 365 AI can segment its customers not just by age or location but by their interaction patterns with the brand, such as frequent online purchases in a specific product category or responsiveness to certain types of marketing content.

Machine learning and predictive analytics

The strength of Dynamics 365 AI lies in its **machine learning** (**ML**) models, which continuously evolve by learning from new data. These models analyze historical customer data to predict future behaviors and preferences. Dynamics 365 AI effectively forecasts trends and buying patterns, enabling businesses to tailor their marketing strategies proactively.

A practical application could be predicting a surge in demand for certain products. Dynamics 365 AI can identify early signs of this trend in customer behavior, allowing businesses to adjust their stock levels and marketing strategies accordingly.

Personalization at scale

Dynamics 365 AI excels in personalizing marketing efforts at a large scale. It enables businesses to create highly customized content and offers for different customer segments. This personalization is data-driven, ensuring that each customer receives marketing material that is most relevant to their interests and behaviors.

For example, Dynamics 365 AI can help a retailer send personalized discount offers on sports equipment to customers who have shown a consistent interest in fitness-related products, thereby increasing the likelihood of purchase.

Real-time campaign adjustments

Dynamics 365 AI's real-time analytics capabilities allow for the dynamic adjustment of marketing campaigns. If a particular campaign is not performing as expected, the AI can quickly analyze feedback and interaction data to adjust the campaign's direction. This agility ensures that marketing efforts are responsive and effective.

Seamless omnichannel marketing integration

An essential feature of Dynamics 365 AI is its ability to integrate seamlessly with omnichannel marketing strategies. It ensures consistent customer segmentation and targeting across all channels, whether it's email, social media, or in-store interactions. This consistency is crucial for a unified customer experience and for reinforcing the marketing message across different platforms.

Ethical considerations in data handling

With great power comes great responsibility. Dynamics 365 AI handles a massive amount of customer data, and with this comes the responsibility to adhere to ethical guidelines and privacy regulations. Dynamics 365 AI is designed with built-in compliance features to ensure businesses can leverage AI capabilities while maintaining customer trust and meeting regulatory requirements.

In conclusion, Dynamics 365 AI is reshaping the way businesses approach customer segmentation and campaign targeting. By offering advanced, AI-driven insights and real-time data analytics, it enables businesses to execute more effective, personalized, and responsive marketing strategies. As we continue to move forward in the digital age, Dynamics 365 AI stands out as an essential tool for businesses looking to innovate and excel in their marketing efforts.

Personalized recommendations and cross-selling opportunities

In today's rapidly evolving digital marketplace, personalization and strategic cross-selling are key differentiators for businesses. Dynamics 365 AI plays a crucial role in this domain, offering robust tools for delivering personalized recommendations and identifying lucrative cross-selling opportunities. This section delves into the sophisticated capabilities of Dynamics 365 AI and how they can be harnessed to enhance sales strategies and customer engagement.

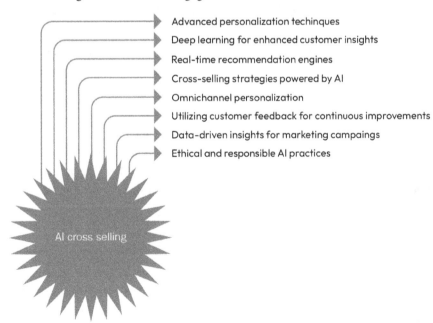

Figure 5.2 – Overview of AI cross selling

Advanced personalization techniques

At the heart of Dynamics 365 AI's personalization capabilities is a complex ML framework. This system processes and analyzes vast amounts of customer data, including transaction histories, browsing patterns, and engagement metrics across various channels. By leveraging this data, Dynamics 365 AI can create detailed customer profiles, which are then used to tailor product recommendations and offers. For example, an online fashion retailer could utilize Dynamics 365 AI to recommend a matching accessory to a customer who has just added a dress to their shopping cart, based on their previous purchases and viewed items.

Deep learning for enhanced customer insights

Dynamics 365 AI employs **deep learning** (**DL**) algorithms to gain nuanced insights into individual customer preferences and behaviors. These insights go beyond simple purchase history; they can include the analysis of customer reviews, ratings, and even social media interactions. By understanding the subtleties of customer preferences, Dynamics 365 AI can curate highly relevant and appealing product recommendations, significantly enhancing the potential for upselling and cross-selling.

Real-time recommendation engines

The real-time recommendation engine in Dynamics 365 AI is a standout feature. As customers interact with a business's digital platforms, the AI system dynamically updates and presents recommendations, making the shopping experience more interactive and responsive. This capability ensures that customers are presented with relevant suggestions at the moment when they are most likely to make a purchase decision.

Cross-selling strategies powered by AI

Dynamics 365 AI enhances cross-selling efforts by intelligently suggesting complementary products and services. By analyzing purchase patterns and customer preferences, the AI can identify products that are frequently bought together or might be of interest to the customer. For instance, a customer purchasing a high-end laptop on an electronics site might be shown recommendations for laptop cases, external hard drives, or premium software subscriptions, enhancing their purchase experience and increasing the **average order value** (**AOV**).

Omnichannel personalization

Dynamics 365 AI's personalization extends across all customer touchpoints, ensuring a consistent and seamless experience whether the customer is shopping online, via a mobile app, or in a physical store. This omnichannel approach to personalization is vital in today's retail environment, where customers expect a unified shopping experience across all platforms.

Utilizing customer feedback for continuous improvement

Dynamics 365 AI also incorporates customer feedback into its learning cycle. Ratings, reviews, and customer feedback are analyzed to continuously refine and improve the recommendation algorithms. This approach ensures that recommendations stay relevant and effective over time, adapting to changing customer preferences and market trends.

Data-driven insights for marketing campaigns

Apart from enhancing individual customer experiences, Dynamics 365 AI provides valuable insights that can inform broader marketing strategies. By analyzing the effectiveness of different recommendation types and customer responses, businesses can tailor their marketing campaigns, promotions, and product development strategies to better meet customer needs.

Ethical and responsible AI practices

In deploying AI for personalization and cross-selling, Dynamics 365 AI adheres to ethical AI principles, ensuring responsible usage of customer data. The platform is designed to comply with data privacy regulations, building trust with customers while leveraging data for business insights.

Personalized recommendations and strategic cross-selling, powered by Dynamics 365 AI, are transforming the way businesses interact with and sell to customers. By delivering tailored suggestions that align with individual customer preferences and behaviors, Dynamics 365 AI not only drives sales but also significantly enhances the customer experience. As we move forward in the digital age, the ability to personalize and strategically cross-sell will continue to be pivotal for businesses seeking to stay competitive and maintain strong customer relationships. Dynamics 365 AI stands as a powerful tool in this endeavor, offering advanced, data-driven solutions for modern, dynamic marketing strategies.

Social media sentiment analysis and brand perception insights

In the digital era, social media is a goldmine of customer insights, and understanding social sentiment is crucial for brand management. Dynamics 365 AI steps into this arena with powerful tools for social media sentiment analysis and brand perception insights. This section explores how Dynamics 365 AI processes and interprets social media data to provide businesses with critical insights into their brand's public perception.

Harnessing social media data

Social media platforms are rich with customer opinions, reviews, and discussions. Dynamics 365 AI taps into this vast resource by aggregating and analyzing data from various social media channels. It employs advanced **natural language processing** (**NLP**) to decipher the tone, context, and sentiment behind social media posts and comments related to a brand or product.

Sentiment analysis and emotional intelligence

At the core of this functionality is sentiment analysis, which categorizes social media content as positive, negative, or neutral. Dynamics 365 AI goes beyond mere keyword analysis; it interprets nuances and context to understand the sentiment accurately. This process involves analyzing linguistic elements such as slang, emojis, and even sarcasm, offering a comprehensive view of public sentiment.

Real-time brand perception tracking

Dynamics 365 AI provides real-time insights into brand perception. Businesses can monitor how their marketing campaigns, product launches, or corporate announcements are being received by the audience. This immediate feedback is invaluable for adjusting strategies, addressing public concerns, or capitalizing on positive sentiment.

Predictive analytics for proactive brand management

Predictive analytics in Dynamics 365 AI enables businesses to foresee potential shifts in brand perception. By analyzing trends and patterns in social sentiment, companies can anticipate and prepare for changes in customer attitudes, allowing for proactive brand management.

Predictive analysis leverages historical data and statistical algorithms to forecast future outcomes. It spans various methods and models, each suited to different types of data, business needs, and predictive goals. Understanding the diversity of predictive analysis techniques is crucial for businesses aiming to make data-driven decisions. Here's an overview of the different types of predictive analysis.

Regression analysis

- **Linear regression**: This method predicts a continuous outcome variable based on one or more predictor variables. It assumes a linear relationship between the predictors and the outcome. Linear regression is widely used for forecasting sales, revenue, and other financial metrics.
- **Logistic regression**: Unlike linear regression, logistic regression is used for binary outcomes (for example, yes/no, win/lose). It estimates the probability of an event occurring, such as customer churn or the likelihood of a loan default.

Time series analysis

Time series analysis forecasts future values based on previously observed values that are time-dependent. It's particularly useful for financial market analysis, economic forecasting, and inventory studies. Time series analysis can account for trends, seasonal variations, and cyclic patterns.

Decision trees

Decision trees are a non-linear predictive modeling technique that divides data into branches to represent different decision paths. They are helpful for classification problems, such as identifying customer segments or predicting which customers are most likely to purchase a particular product.

Random forests

An extension of decision trees, random forests use multiple decision trees to improve prediction accuracy. By aggregating the outcomes of various trees, random forests reduce the risk of overfitting and are powerful for both classification and regression tasks.

Neural networks and DL

Neural networks (**NNs**), inspired by the human brain's structure, are particularly adept at processing complex patterns in large datasets. DL, a subset of NNs, uses multiple layers of processing to extract features and perform classification tasks. These methods are excellent for image and speech recognition, NLP, and sophisticated time series forecasting.

Support vector machines

Support vector machines (**SVMs**) are a set of **supervised learning** (**SL**) methods used for classification and regression analysis. An SVM can model non-linear relationships and is particularly useful in high-dimensional spaces, making it effective for text classification, image recognition, and bioinformatics.

Ensemble methods

Ensemble methods, such as boosting and bagging, combine predictions from multiple models to improve accuracy. For instance, gradient boosting adjusts for errors in previous models, with new models focusing on difficult-to-predict instances. Ensemble methods are versatile, enhancing the performance of both classification and regression models.

Clustering techniques

Though not predictive in the traditional sense, clustering techniques such as K-means or hierarchical clustering can inform predictive models by identifying natural groupings within data. These insights can then inform targeted predictive models for more nuanced forecasting.

Anomaly detection

Anomaly detection identifies outliers in data that do not fit expected patterns. This is crucial for fraud detection, network security, and detecting system failures. Techniques range from statistical methods to complex ML algorithms.

Survival analysis

Survival analysis models time-to-event data, focusing on the duration until an event occurs. It's widely used in medical research to evaluate treatment effectiveness, in engineering for reliability analysis, and in customer analytics for predicting churn.

Each type of predictive analysis has its strengths and applications, and the choice among them depends on the specific business question, the nature of the data available, and the desired outcome. A nuanced understanding of these methods enables businesses to harness their data effectively, unlocking insights that drive strategic decisions and competitive advantage.

Incorporating customer feedback into strategy

The insights gained from social media sentiment analysis are not just for immediate reaction but also for long-term strategy. Dynamics 365 AI helps businesses understand customer expectations and preferences, guiding product development, marketing strategies, and customer service approaches.

Case study – Retail brand leverages social sentiment analysis

A leading retail brand used Dynamics 365 AI to analyze social sentiment during a major product launch. By monitoring real-time social media discussions, they identified a concern about product sustainability. Quickly addressing this through targeted communication and policy changes, they improved public perception and avoided a potential PR crisis.

Best practices in social media sentiment analysis

The effective use of social media sentiment analysis involves several best practices, as depicted in the following diagram:

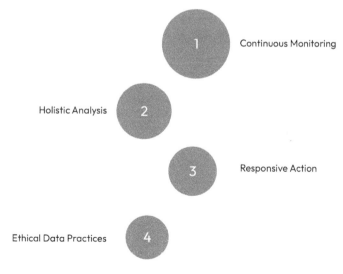

Figure 5.3 – Best practices for social media sentiment analysis

Let's look at these in more detail:

1. **Continuous monitoring**: Regularly track social sentiment, not just during specific campaigns or events.

2. **Holistic analysis**: Consider sentiment analysis as part of a broader market research strategy, combining it with other data sources for a complete picture.

3. **Responsive action**: Be prepared to respond quickly to negative sentiment while also amplifying positive trends.

4. **Ethical data practices**: Ensure compliance with data privacy regulations and ethical standards in data collection and analysis.

Social media sentiment analysis and brand perception insights offered by Dynamics 365 AI are invaluable tools in today's digital marketing landscape. They provide businesses with a real-time pulse of public opinion, enabling them to manage their brand proactively and responsively. By leveraging these tools, companies can not only protect and enhance their brand image but also align their strategies more closely with customer needs and market trends. As social media continues to be a dominant platform for customer expression, the role of AI in interpreting and leveraging this data will become increasingly crucial for businesses worldwide.

Real-world examples and best practices in marketing insights

In demonstrating the practical applications of Dynamics 365 AI in marketing, this section delves into three complex and detailed use cases. Each case study showcases the strategic implementation of AI-driven marketing insights and the resultant business transformations.

Example 1 – Hyper-personalized campaigns by a fashion e-commerce platform

Background: A leading e-commerce platform specializing in fashion sought to refine its marketing approach by moving beyond generic demographic-based targeting.

Application of Dynamics 365 AI

Leveraging Dynamics 365 AI, the platform developed a multi-tiered customer segmentation model. This model used AI to analyze customer data, including past purchases, browsing behavior, and social media interactions. Dynamics 365 AI identified not only broad segments but also micro-segments within their customer base, such as "eco-conscious buyers" or "trend-driven young adults."

Outcome

Utilizing these micro-segments, the platform launched hyper-personalized marketing campaigns. For example, eco-conscious buyers received curated selections of sustainable fashion items. This approach led to a 45% increase in customer engagement rates and a 25% rise in sales within these segments. The detailed segmentation also enabled the platform to identify emerging fashion trends, gaining a competitive edge in the market.

Example 2 – Optimized patient outreach by a healthcare provider network

Background: A healthcare provider network aimed to enhance its patient engagement and preventive care programs.

Application of Dynamics 365 AI

The network used Dynamics 365 AI to analyze patient data, including health history, engagement with previous outreach programs, and demographic information. AI helped identify patients who would most benefit from specific preventive care programs.

Outcome

Tailored outreach campaigns were developed for different patient groups. For instance, patients with a history of chronic illnesses received personalized reminders and educational content about managing their conditions. This targeted approach resulted in a 30% increase in patient enrollment in preventive care programs and a significant improvement in patient health outcomes.

Example 3 – Market expansion strategy for a SaaS company

Background: A **Software-as-a-Service** (**SaaS**) company wanted to expand its market reach into new industries.

Application of Dynamics 365 AI

The company utilized Dynamics 365 AI to conduct a thorough market analysis, identifying industries where their software could address specific pain points. The AI system analyzed industry trends, competitor presence, and potential customer needs.

Outcome

Based on AI insights, the company developed customized software solutions for targeted industries, such as healthcare and education, and launched industry-specific marketing campaigns. This strategic approach led to successful market penetration, with a 50% increase in client acquisition in these new sectors and a notable rise in brand recognition within these industries.

Best practices for leveraging marketing insights with Dynamics 365 AI

- **Comprehensive data integration**: Ensure that all customer interaction points are integrated into Dynamics 365 AI for a complete view of customer behavior
- **Continuous model training and updating**: Regularly update the AI models with new data and feedback to keep insights relevant and accurate
- **Ethical data usage**: Adhere to data privacy laws and ethical standards, ensuring customer data is used responsibly and transparently
- **Cross-functional collaboration**: Collaborate across marketing, sales, and IT departments to effectively utilize AI insights in comprehensive marketing strategies
- **Monitor and adapt strategies**: Continuously monitor the performance of AI-driven campaigns and be ready to adapt strategies based on real-time data and changing market dynamics

The detailed use cases and outlined best practices demonstrate the vast potential of Dynamics 365 AI in transforming marketing strategies. By adopting a data-driven approach, companies can achieve more personalized, effective, and efficient marketing efforts. These real-world examples serve as a guide for businesses looking to harness the power of AI for marketing optimization, providing a roadmap to enhanced customer engagement and business success.

Summary

As we conclude our exploration into the transformative world of AI-driven marketing, it's evident that Dynamics 365 AI has become a cornerstone in reshaping how businesses approach and execute their marketing strategies. Throughout this journey, we have delved into the intricate workings of AI in customer segmentation, campaign targeting, personalized recommendations, and the critical role of social media sentiment analysis in brand perception.

The advanced capabilities of Dynamics 365 AI in dissecting and analyzing complex customer data have unlocked new dimensions in customer segmentation. By moving beyond traditional demographics to include behavioral and psychographic factors, businesses can now target their marketing efforts with unprecedented precision. This refined targeting not only maximizes the impact of campaigns but also ensures effective resource utilization.

The shift toward personalized customer experiences, powered by Dynamics 365 AI, marks a new era in customer engagement. By leveraging predictive analytics to offer tailor-made product suggestions, businesses are transforming casual browsers into loyal customers, thereby deepening customer relationships and opening new avenues for revenue generation.

The role of Dynamics 365 AI in monitoring and interpreting the vast and complex world of social media has been particularly impactful. Real-time analysis of sentiments and trends offers businesses an immediate understanding of their brand's standing, enabling them to adjust strategies swiftly and maintain a positive brand image in the digital domain.

Real-world examples from various industries, from fashion retail to healthcare, demonstrated the practical application and success of AI-driven marketing strategies. These case studies not only validated the effectiveness of AI in marketing but also served as a valuable source of best practices and insights.

Key practices such as comprehensive data integration, continuous model training, ethical data usage, cross-functional collaboration, and the adaptability of marketing strategies based on real-time data have emerged as essential in maximizing the benefits of AI in marketing.

In summary, the integration of AI in marketing, particularly through Dynamics 365 AI, is not merely an enhancement of existing practices but a necessary evolution to stay competitive in an increasingly digital world. As AI continues to advance, its influence in shaping effective, personalized, and dynamic marketing strategies becomes increasingly indispensable. This exploration serves as a testament to the power of AI in marketing, offering a glimpse into a future where marketing strategies are more adaptable, insightful, and customer-centric than ever before.

The next chapter addresses AI's role in financial analytics, including how AI improves financial forecasting and fraud detection programs and helps manage financial risks.

Questions

1. How does Dynamics 365 AI enhance customer segmentation for marketing purposes?

2. What role does predictive analytics play in personalized recommendations offered by Dynamics 365 AI?

3. How does Dynamics 365 AI utilize social media sentiment analysis for brand perception?

4. What are some key best practices for leveraging AI in marketing, as discussed in the chapter?

Answers

1. Dynamics 365 AI enhances customer segmentation by analyzing extensive customer data, including purchasing patterns, online behavior, and social media interactions. It goes beyond traditional demographics to identify specific customer groups based on behaviors, preferences, and needs, enabling more targeted and effective marketing campaigns.

2. Predictive analytics in Dynamics 365 AI analyzes past customer data to anticipate future buying behaviors and preferences. This allows businesses to offer personalized product suggestions and recommendations, enhancing customer experience and increasing the likelihood of sales.

3. Dynamics 365 AI uses social media sentiment analysis to monitor and interpret public opinions and discussions about a brand on social media platforms. It employs NLP to categorize sentiments as positive, negative, or neutral, providing real-time insights into the brand's public perception and enabling businesses to adjust their strategies accordingly.

4. Key best practices include comprehensive data integration across customer touchpoints, continuous training and updating of AI models, adherence to ethical data usage and privacy laws, fostering cross-functional collaboration between departments, and regularly monitoring and adapting marketing strategies based on real-time AI-driven insights.

6

Financial Analytics with Dynamics 365 AI

In the intricate world of financial management and strategy, precision, foresight, and adaptability are paramount. In this chapter, we'll delve into the transformative role of AI in revolutionizing financial processes within businesses. As we navigate the rapidly evolving economic landscapes, Dynamics 365 AI emerges as a critical tool, enabling more accurate financial forecasting, robust fraud detection, and effective risk management strategies.

The first section on *AI-powered financial forecasting and budgeting*, explores how Dynamics 365 AI leverages predictive analytics and machine learning algorithms to enhance financial planning and analysis. Traditional financial forecasting methods often involve a considerable amount of guesswork and are vulnerable to human error. However, AI introduces a level of precision and adaptability previously unattainable. This section will discuss how Dynamics 365 AI analyzes historical data and market trends to predict future financial scenarios, helping businesses plan budgets more effectively and make informed financial decisions.

Moving on to the second section, the focus shifts to *fraud detection and prevention using advanced analytics*. In an era where financial fraud schemes are becoming increasingly sophisticated, traditional detection methods are often inadequate. This section will illustrate how Dynamics 365 AI employs pattern recognition and anomaly detection techniques to identify suspicious activities. By continuously learning from new data, AI systems can adapt to emerging fraud tactics, providing businesses with a dynamic defense mechanism against financial threats.

In the third section, we'll address *risk assessment and mitigation strategies*. Here, the spotlight will be on how Dynamics 365 AI aids businesses in identifying, assessing, and mitigating various types of financial risks. From market volatility to credit risk, AI provides a comprehensive toolkit for analyzing potential threats and devising strategies to minimize their impact. This section will explore the multifaceted approach to risk management, highlighting how AI contributes to building financial resilience and stability.

Finally, this chapter will reemphasize and further explore *risk assessment and mitigation strategies*, diving deeper into practical applications and strategic implications. It will detail how businesses can implement these AI-driven strategies to not only respond to risks reactively but also to anticipate and prepare for them proactively.

Throughout this chapter, current and emerging trends in AI financial analytics will be examined, reflecting the latest advancements and best practices in the field. As businesses seek to navigate the complexities of modern finance, Dynamics 365 AI stands as an essential ally, transforming data into actionable insights and empowering financial leaders to steer their organizations toward growth and stability with confidence. This chapter aims to equip you with a comprehensive understanding of the potential and practicalities of leveraging Dynamics 365 AI for advanced financial analytics, paving the way for more strategic and informed financial decision-making.

Here is the list of the topics that will be covered:

- Enhanced financial forecasting and budgeting with AI
- Enhanced fraud detection and prevention using advanced analytics with Dynamics 365 AI
- Revolutionizing risk assessment and mitigation strategies
- Dynamics 365 AI – transforming financial operations

Enhanced financial forecasting and budgeting with AI

The advent of AI in financial forecasting and budgeting is creating a paradigm shift in how businesses approach their financial strategies and operations. With Dynamics 365 AI, companies are not only equipped to handle vast amounts of financial data but are also empowered to draw sophisticated, actionable insights from it. Let's delve into the technicalities of AI's impact on financial forecasting and budgeting and the consequent business implications.

Technical sophistication in predictive analytics

Dynamics 365 AI incorporates complex machine learning algorithms and statistical models to conduct predictive analytics, going far beyond traditional linear regressions. These models include time series analysis, neural networks, and ensemble methods that can handle non-linear patterns, seasonality, and volatility in financial data. For instance, by applying these advanced techniques, businesses can anticipate cash flow shortages or surpluses, demand fluctuations, and even the impact of regulatory changes on financial performance. The technical sophistication of these models means forecasts are not only more accurate but also provide a range of probable outcomes with associated risks, helping businesses plan for various contingencies.

Automation in budgeting processes

AI streamlines the budgeting process through automation, dramatically reducing the time and resources traditionally required. It integrates and analyzes data from across business functions – sales, operations, HR, and so on – and external sources such as market indices or economic reports. **Natural language processing** (**NLP**) capabilities allow it to include insights from textual data such as market news or financial reports. By automating the data collection and preliminary analysis processes, AI enables finance professionals to focus on strategic decision-making and scenario analysis. Additionally, AI systems can continuously monitor financial performance against the budget, providing real-time alerts and recommendations for adjustments, ensuring that businesses remain agile and responsive.

Dynamic and adaptive financial planning

AI's real-time data processing capabilities allow for dynamic financial planning. Unlike static models, AI systems constantly update forecasts as new data becomes available, reflecting the latest market conditions and internal performance metrics. This means businesses can quickly adapt to changes, seizing opportunities or mitigating risks promptly. Moreover, AI's ability to learn and adapt over time means that financial models become increasingly accurate and tailored to the specific business environment and strategy, continually improving the quality of financial insights.

Scenario planning and risk assessment

AI enhances scenario planning by enabling a vast array of financial scenarios to be simulated based on various internal and external variables. Through techniques such as Monte Carlo simulations or stress testing, businesses can assess the financial implications of different scenarios, understanding potential risks and opportunities. This capability is particularly valuable in uncertain or volatile markets, where businesses need to be prepared for a range of possible outcomes. By providing a probabilistic assessment of various scenarios, AI aids in crafting robust risk mitigation and contingency strategies.

Business impacts and considerations

The technical enhancements brought by AI in financial forecasting and budgeting have several business implications. Improved accuracy and timeliness of financial insights lead to better strategic decisions and operational efficiency. Dynamic and adaptive planning capabilities mean businesses can remain competitive and resilient in the face of market changes. However, the integration of AI also requires businesses to invest in data infrastructure and analytics capabilities and to adopt a culture that embraces data-driven decision-making. Additionally, reliance on AI for financial decisions necessitates a clear understanding of the models' workings and limitations, ensuring that insights are interpreted correctly and ethically.

In summary, AI's introduction to financial forecasting and budgeting is not merely an incremental change but a transformative shift. Dynamics 365 AI's capabilities enable businesses to navigate the complexities of modern finance more effectively, turning financial planning from a periodic exercise into a continuous, integral part of the business strategy. With increased technical sophistication, businesses can expect not only to react to financial changes but also to anticipate and prepare for future financial landscapes.

Enhanced fraud detection and prevention using advanced analytics with Dynamics 365 AI

In an era marked by increasingly sophisticated financial fraud, Dynamics 365 AI offers an advanced suite of tools and techniques designed to detect and prevent fraudulent activities. This section delves deeper into how Dynamics 365 AI employs complex analytics to provide robust fraud protection mechanisms.

Employing a multifaceted analytical approach for detection

Dynamics 365 AI doesn't rely on a single method but combines various advanced analytical techniques to detect fraudulent activities. These include the following:

- **Anomaly detection**: This technique identifies unusual patterns that deviate significantly from established normal behaviors. Dynamics 365 AI utilizes sophisticated anomaly detection algorithms that consider a multitude of factors, such as transaction size, frequency, and the network of entities involved. For instance, it can flag unusually large transactions or a high volume of transactions in a short time, which are often indicators of fraudulent activities.

- **Predictive modeling**: Dynamics 365 AI uses predictive modeling to identify potential fraud before it happens. By analyzing historical data, including known instances of fraud, AI can learn to predict future fraudulent transactions. These models are continuously refined as they are exposed to new data, making the predictions more accurate over time.

- **Network analysis**: This technique is particularly effective in exposing complex fraud schemes involving multiple parties or accounts. Dynamics 365 AI analyzes the connections between different entities, looking for suspicious patterns and relationships. For example, it might identify a network of accounts with irregular transaction patterns, which may suggest money laundering activities.

Machine learning for dynamic and adaptive fraud detection

Machine learning is a cornerstone of AI's capability in fraud detection, enabling systems to learn from past data and improve over time. Dynamics 365 AI uses the following:

- **Supervised learning**: Here, the system is trained on a dataset labeled as fraudulent or legitimate, allowing it to learn the characteristics of fraud

- **Unsupervised learning**: Here, the system identifies anomalies and potential fraud by detecting patterns and outliers in data without pre-labeled instances

- **Reinforcement learning**: Here, the system continuously improves its detection strategies based on feedback from its successes and failures in fraud detection

These learning models ensure that the AI system remains effective against evolving and previously unseen fraud tactics.

Seamless integration with organizational data systems

For effective fraud detection, AI needs to have a holistic view of the organization's data. Dynamics 365 AI integrates seamlessly with various data sources, including transactional systems, customer databases, and external data feeds. This integration allows AI to analyze data from multiple perspectives and detect fraud that might be overlooked if the data sources were siloed.

Real-time detection and automated intervention

Dynamics 365 AI provides the capability to detect fraudulent activities in real time and take immediate action. It can automatically flag suspicious transactions for review, block transactions, or even reverse actions if fraud is detected. The system can also be configured to notify human investigators for further analysis, combining AI efficiency with human judgment.

Navigating ethical terrain and ensuring compliance

While implementing advanced AI for fraud detection, businesses must navigate the ethical and legal terrain carefully. This includes ensuring customer data privacy, addressing potential biases in AI algorithms, and adhering to all relevant regulations and standards. Dynamics 365 AI is designed with compliance and ethical considerations in mind, providing tools for transparency, auditability, and control over AI functionalities.

In conclusion, the sophisticated analytics capabilities of Dynamics 365 AI provide a comprehensive and adaptive approach to fraud detection and prevention. By integrating various analytical techniques, machine learning models, and real-time detection capabilities, Dynamics 365 AI helps businesses safeguard their assets and maintain trust with customers and stakeholders. As financial fraud tactics continue to evolve, so too will the AI strategies designed to combat them, making Dynamics 365 AI an essential tool in the fight against fraud.

Revolutionizing risk assessment and mitigation strategies

Risk management is a critical cornerstone for any business seeking longevity and stability. With the advent of Dynamics 365 AI, companies are now equipped to approach risk assessment and mitigation with unprecedented sophistication and foresight. Let's delve deeper into how each facet of risk management is enhanced by the advanced capabilities of Dynamics 365 AI.

Enhanced risk identification through deep data analysis

Identifying risks accurately is the first line of defense for any organization. Dynamics 365 AI elevates this process by providing the following:

- **Comprehensive data aggregation**: AI systems consolidate data from a wide array of sources, including internal financial records, customer feedback, market trends, and even geopolitical events. This broad spectrum of data provides a more nuanced view of potential risks.

- **Advanced pattern and anomaly detection**: Employing sophisticated algorithms, Dynamics 365 AI scrutinizes data for unusual patterns and anomalies that human analysts might miss. For example, it can detect irregular financial transactions that may indicate embezzlement or fraud, or it might identify unexpected changes in customer purchase behavior, indicating a shift in market trends.

Detailed risk analysis and quantification

Once potential risks have been identified, understanding their nature and potential impact is crucial. Dynamics 365 AI makes this process more robust by providing the following:

- **Multi-dimensional risk modeling**: AI doesn't just look at a single aspect of risk; it builds multi-dimensional models that consider various factors and their interrelations. This might include the volatility of market conditions, sensitivity to certain economic changes, or exposure to regulatory shifts.

- **Predictive risk scoring**: Beyond current risk analysis, AI predicts future risk scenarios using historical data and predictive modeling. It assigns risk scores based on the predicted severity and likelihood of various threats, helping organizations prioritize their mitigation efforts effectively.

Strategic mitigation with AI insights

With a thorough understanding of risks, businesses need to strategize their mitigation efforts effectively. Dynamics 365 AI facilitates this in the following ways:

- **Scenario planning and simulations**: AI can simulate a wide range of scenarios under different conditions to see how various risks might affect the organization. This helps in creating flexible and robust mitigation strategies.

- **Optimization algorithms for mitigation planning**: AI helps in determining the most effective risk mitigation strategies, balancing the potential impact with resource allocation. It can recommend whether to avoid, accept, transfer, or mitigate specific risks based on the organization's risk tolerance and objectives.

Adaptive monitoring for ongoing risk management

Effective risk management is continuous. Dynamics 365 AI supports this need by providing the following:

- **Real-time monitoring and alerts**: The system keeps a vigilant eye on risk indicators and provides real-time alerts when certain thresholds are breached, allowing for swift action.

- **Feedback loops for learning and adaptation**: AI systems improve over time through feedback loops. They learn from every new piece of data and every risk event encountered, continuously enhancing their predictive accuracy and response strategies.

Ethical and regulatory adherence in AI-driven risk management

Incorporating AI into risk management brings its own set of ethical and compliance considerations. Dynamics 365 AI addresses this through the following aspects:

- **Transparency in AI decision-making**: Dynamics 365 AI aims to make its decision-making process as transparent as possible, providing clear explanations for risk assessments and recommendations. This transparency is crucial for maintaining trust and accountability.

- **Compliance tools and features**: Dynamics 365 AI includes features to help organizations comply with various regulatory requirements related to risk management. This includes tools for data governance, audit trails, and reporting mechanisms.

In conclusion, Dynamics 365 AI significantly refines each aspect of risk management, from identification and analysis to mitigation and ongoing monitoring. By offering deep insights, predictive capabilities, and continuous learning, Dynamics 365 AI not only enhances an organization's ability to manage current risks but also prepares it to face future challenges more effectively. As businesses continue to operate in an increasingly complex and uncertain environment, the advanced risk management capabilities provided by Dynamics 365 AI will become even more integral to their success and resilience.

Dynamics 365 AI – transforming financial operations

As businesses navigate an increasingly complex financial landscape, Dynamics 365 AI emerges as a critical tool for enhancing accuracy, efficiency, and strategic insight. This section will provide detailed case studies illustrating the transformative impact of Dynamics 365 AI in financial operations, emphasizing the challenges faced and the strategic solutions implemented.

Case study 1 – forecasting accuracy in a multinational corporation

Background and challenge: A multinational corporation was facing the challenge of creating accurate financial forecasts due to the complexity of its global operations and rapidly changing market conditions. The existing forecasting methods were time-consuming and often resulted in outdated or inaccurate predictions:

- **Implementation**: The corporation implemented Dynamics 365 AI to integrate data across various business units and employ machine learning algorithms for predictive analysis. The AI system was tasked with analyzing patterns in historical financial data, market trends, and operational metrics.

- **Outcomes**: Dynamics 365 AI dramatically improved the accuracy and timeliness of financial forecasts. The predictive models adapted to new data, allowing for real-time updates and adjustments to forecasts. As a result, the corporation benefited from more reliable strategic planning and resource allocation, enhancing its agility and market responsiveness.

Case study 2 – banking on AI to combat fraud

Background and challenge: A leading bank was combating an increase in sophisticated fraud attempts, threatening customer assets and trust. Traditional fraud detection systems were not keeping pace with the sophisticated tactics employed by fraudsters, leading to a high rate of false positives and undetected fraud:

- **Implementation**: The bank integrated Dynamics 365 AI into its monitoring systems, utilizing advanced analytics for anomaly detection and pattern recognition. The AI system was trained on historical transaction data, including known fraud instances, to identify markers of fraudulent activity.

- **Outcomes**: The new AI-driven system significantly improved the detection of fraudulent transactions while reducing false positives. It provided real-time alerts and the capability to adapt to new fraud patterns, thereby protecting customer assets and enhancing trust. The bank also saw an increase in operational efficiency since the AI system automated much of the fraud detection process.

Case study 3 – risk management reinvented for an investment firm

Background and challenge: An investment firm was seeking ways to better manage and mitigate the risks associated with its diverse portfolio, especially in light of unpredictable market volatility. Traditional risk assessment methods were not providing the depth or speed of analysis required for proactive risk management:

- **Implementation**: The firm employed Dynamics 365 AI to conduct comprehensive risk analysis and scenario planning. The system analyzed vast quantities of market data, investment trends, and economic indicators to assess and predict potential risks, providing a multi-faceted view of possible future market scenarios.

- **Outcomes**: The AI-enhanced risk management approach allowed the firm to identify risks more proactively and develop targeted strategies to mitigate them. The continuous learning capability of AI meant that the firm could adjust its strategies in real time, ensuring a resilient and adaptive investment approach. This led to improved portfolio performance and investor confidence.

These case studies provide a snapshot of how Dynamics 365 AI is revolutionizing financial forecasting, fraud detection, and risk management. Each story highlights not only the challenges faced by organizations in maintaining robust financial operations but also the innovative ways in which Dynamics 365 AI provides solutions. Through enhanced predictive analytics, real-time data processing, and adaptive learning capabilities, Dynamics 365 AI empowers businesses to navigate the complexities of the financial world with greater confidence and strategic acumen. As businesses continue to face an array of financial challenges, the role of Dynamics 365 AI in enabling more informed, efficient, and proactive financial management becomes ever more pertinent.

As we conclude our exploration of *Financial Analytics with Dynamics 365 AI*, it's clear that AI has fundamentally transformed how businesses approach their financial strategy and operations. Throughout this chapter, we've seen the myriad ways in which Dynamics 365 AI is empowering businesses to harness predictive insights for financial forecasting, safeguard assets through advanced fraud detection techniques, and embrace sophisticated risk management strategies.

Summary

The journey has shown us that AI-powered financial forecasting and budgeting is not just about enhancing accuracy; it's about redefining efficiency and strategic foresight in financial planning. By leveraging vast amounts of data and employing advanced machine learning algorithms, Dynamics 365 AI provides businesses with the tools to anticipate future market trends and customer needs, allowing for proactive and informed decision-making.

In the realm of fraud detection, Dynamics 365 AI stands as a vigilant sentinel, employing anomaly detection and pattern recognition to identify and prevent fraudulent activities. This AI-enhanced vigilance is crucial in an era where financial fraud tactics are constantly evolving, ensuring that businesses can protect their reputation and customer trust.

Risk management has also been reimagined through the lens of AI. Dynamics 365 AI enables businesses to identify and assess risks with a new level of precision and depth. By simulating various scenarios and analyzing potential impacts, businesses can prepare and strategize effectively, turning potential threats into opportunities for growth and stability.

The real-world case studies presented in this chapter serve as a testament to the transformative potential of Dynamics 365 AI across various sectors. They provide not just a glimpse into the successful implementation of AI in financial operations but also act as a source of inspiration and practical insight for businesses looking to embark on their journeys of financial transformation.

In the next chapter, *Leveraging Generative AI in Dynamics 365*, we'll be on the cusp of diving deeper into the innovative realm of AI. Generative AI promises to further expand the capabilities and applications of AI in business, offering new and exciting ways to create, innovate, and deliver value.

In summary, this chapter has laid a foundational understanding of the significant role AI plays in modern financial analytics. As businesses continue to navigate a complex and ever-changing financial landscape, Dynamics 365 AI provides the tools and insights needed for them to thrive. The journey into AI-enhanced financial operations is just beginning, and the potential for growth and innovation is boundless. As we move forward, the lessons and insights from this chapter will undoubtedly serve as guiding principles for embracing and leveraging the power of AI in finance.

The next chapter will address how to leverage generative AI in Dynamics 365.

Questions

1. How does Dynamics 365 AI enhance financial forecasting and budgeting for businesses?

2. What are some ways Dynamics 365 AI contributes to fraud detection and prevention?

3. In what ways does Dynamics 365 AI assist businesses in managing and mitigating risks?

4. How does continuous learning and adaptation in Dynamics 365 AI influence its effectiveness in financial operations over time?

Answers

1. Dynamics 365 AI enhances financial forecasting and budgeting by utilizing predictive analytics and machine learning algorithms to analyze historical and current data, identify patterns, and predict future financial scenarios. This allows businesses to make informed decisions, allocate resources more effectively, and adapt swiftly to market changes.

2. Dynamics 365 AI contributes to fraud detection and prevention by employing advanced techniques such as anomaly detection and pattern recognition. It analyzes transactions and user behavior to identify unusual patterns that may indicate fraudulent activity. By continuously learning from new data, it adapts to emerging fraud tactics, providing businesses with a dynamic and effective defense mechanism.

3. Dynamics 365 AI assists in risk management by providing comprehensive tools for risk assessment and mitigation strategies. It uses predictive analytics to forecast potential risks and their impacts on business operations. AI also aids in scenario planning, allowing businesses to prepare for various outcomes and develop strategies to mitigate identified risks effectively.

4. Continuous learning and adaptation are fundamental features of Dynamics 365 AI that significantly enhance its effectiveness in financial operations over time. As the AI system is exposed to more data, including new financial transactions, market trends, and outcomes of previous predictions, it refines its algorithms and improves its predictive accuracy. This means the system becomes better at forecasting financial outcomes, detecting fraudulent activities, and assessing risks, ensuring that financial strategies and protective measures evolve in line with the changing business landscape and regulatory environment. This continuous improvement cycle helps businesses stay ahead of potential financial challenges and capitalize on emerging opportunities more effectively.

Part 3: Advanced Applications and Future Directions

This part of the book dives deep into the advanced applications and strategic implementations of Dynamics 365 AI, guiding you through the cutting-edge aspects of artificial intelligence in business environments. From exploring the realm of generative AI to harnessing the capabilities of MS Copilot, and from deploying AI-driven virtual agents for customer service to implementing robust fraud protection strategies, these chapters provide a detailed look at the sophisticated use cases of Dynamics 365 AI. The aim is to equip you with the knowledge and insights needed to leverage these advanced AI tools, thereby driving innovation, efficiency, and security in their organizations. Whether it's through enhancing customer interactions, protecting against fraudulent activities, or optimizing operations with intelligent insights, this part of the book is designed to showcase the breadth of possibilities that Dynamics 365 AI offers for businesses ready to embrace the next level of AI-driven transformation.

This part has the following chapters:

- *Chapter 7, Leveraging Generative AI in Dynamics 365*

- *Chapter 8, Harnessing MS Copilot for Enhanced Business Insights*

- *Chapter 9, "Virtual Agent for Customer Service" in the Context of MS Copilot and Microsoft Dynamics*

- *Chapter 10, Fraud Protection with Dynamics 365 AI*

7

Leveraging Generative AI in Dynamics 365

In the evolving landscape of digital transformation, this chapter embarks on an insightful journey into the integration and application of generative AI within the Dynamics 365 ecosystem. This chapter is meticulously crafted to demystify the concept of generative AI and illustrate its transformative impact across diverse business operations, offering a nuanced understanding of its potential to enhance business insights and intelligent decision-making.

We begin by unraveling the essence of generative AI, a branch of artificial intelligence that is redefining the boundaries of data utilization and content creation. This segment of the chapter delves into the mechanics of how generative AI, through advanced machine learning models such as GPT-3 and GPT-4, processes vast datasets to generate human-like, contextually relevant text. The exploration extends to uncovering the myriad applications of this technology—from automating routine tasks and generating insightful reports to creating innovative solutions for complex problems. The aim is to illuminate how generative AI is not just an incremental advancement but a revolutionary leap in business technology.

The narrative then transitions to a comprehensive overview of OpenAI and Azure Open AI Service. This section offers a closer look at the journey of OpenAI, highlighting its groundbreaking advancements in AI research and development. It further examines the synergy between OpenAI's cutting-edge models and Azure's robust cloud computing platform, elucidating how this integration marks a significant collaboration in the realm of technology, offering powerful AI capabilities at scale.

As the chapter progresses, we delve into the intricacies of integrating generative AI into Dynamics 365 AI. This discussion focuses on how the latest language models and tools, such as ChatGPT, can be seamlessly woven into the fabric of Dynamics 365. The chapter provides technical insights into how these models enhance customer interaction, streamline communication processes, and drive operational efficiency. It's a narrative about transforming business applications with AI, ensuring that every interaction and decision is backed by intelligent, data-driven insights.

To anchor the theoretical and technical discussions in reality, the chapter concludes with a series of real-world use cases and implementation examples. These stories are carefully selected to demonstrate how businesses from various sectors have successfully harnessed the power of generative AI within Dynamics 365 to solve unique challenges, improve customer engagement, and innovate in their respective fields. Each case study is a testament to the practical applications of generative AI, offering valuable lessons and strategic approaches that businesses can adopt.

In summary, this chapter is not just an exploration of generative AI's capabilities but also a guide to implementing and leveraging these advanced technologies in business operations. It provides readers with a detailed understanding of how generative AI can be used to unlock new levels of efficiency, creativity, and customer engagement within the Dynamics 365 platform. As businesses continue to navigate the digital era, the insights from this chapter will be instrumental in shaping their journey toward a more intelligent, AI-integrated future.

Here's a list of the topics covered in the chapter:

- The mechanism behind generative AI – An in-depth technical exploration
- Azure Open AI Service: An in-depth technical exploration
- Integrating language models and ChatGPT with Dynamics 365 AI
- Real-world use cases and implementation examples of integrating language models and ChatGPT with Dynamics 365 AI

The mechanism behind generative AI – An in-depth technical exploration

Generative AI stands at the cutting edge of artificial intelligence, where complex neural network architectures are designed not just to analyze data but to create it. This capability is largely driven by **generative adversarial networks** (**GANs**) and advanced deep learning models such as the Transformer architecture used in language processing.

This section delves into the realm of advanced neural networks within GANs and transformer-based models, spotlighting their pivotal roles in shaping the future of artificial intelligence. It covers the intricacies of the generator and discriminator mechanisms of GANs, their adversarial training dynamics, and computational demands, as well as the transformative impact of transformers in language generation and processing. This exploration not only highlights the technical sophistication and potential applications in enhancing business processes but also addresses the challenges and ethical considerations involved in deploying these cutting-edge technologies.

Advanced neural networks in GANs

The core components of GANs are the generator and discriminator networks in their collaborative yet competitive framework:

- **GAN architecture**: A GAN comprises two distinct but interconnected neural networks—the generator and the discriminator. These networks function in a state of adversarial competition, where the success of one directly influences the other.

- **The generator**: By operating as the creative force, the generator network starts from the point of random noise and gradually learns to generate data (images, text, etc.) that mimic real-world inputs. This process involves complex layers of neural networks that progressively refine the output, making it increasingly realistic. For example, in an application designed to create new artwork, the generator might initially produce abstract shapes and colors. Over time, and through the training process, it begins to generate images that resemble recognizable artistic styles, such as impressionist landscapes or portraits, by refining its understanding of the elements that make these styles unique. This evolution showcases the generator's ability to start from randomness and advance towards creating sophisticated, life-like art.

- **The discriminator**: As the arbiter of authenticity, the discriminator network analyzes both the outputs from the generator and actual data from the training set. Its objective is to accurately classify the inputs as either real or fake, effectively "teaching" the generator to improve its output. For instance, in the context of image generation, if the discriminator is presented with both computer-generated images of landscapes and genuine photographs from a dataset, it must determine which images are AI-created and which are real. This process pressures the generator to produce increasingly convincing landscape images, narrowing the gap between artificial and authentic visuals.

Training dynamics and computational aspects

We can explore GANs by focusing on their adversarial training process, their challenges in achieving convergence and stability, and the computational resources they require.

- **Adversarial training process**: The training of GANs is a sophisticated dance between the generator and discriminator. Through iterative cycles of training, the generator strives to produce more authentic outputs while the discriminator continuously hones its ability to distinguish genuine from generated data.

- **Convergence and stability**: Achieving convergence in a GAN, where the generator produces high-fidelity outputs and the discriminator has a 50% detection rate (akin to guessing), is complex. It involves the careful tuning of the neural networks and learning rates to maintain stability and prevent mode collapse.

- **Computational load**: GANs demand significant computational power, attributed to the complexity of their architecture and the extensive training data required. Training these models often involves sophisticated GPUs and parallel computing resources.

Generative AI in text and language processing

The development of transformer-based models, particularly GPT-3 and its predecessors, has marked a revolution in generative AI for text and language processing.

Transformer architecture and language understanding

Transformer architecture utilizing deep learning showcases its unique self-attention mechanisms for intricate language comprehension and its scalable design that excels in contextual learning, thereby setting a new standard in NLP capabilities.

- **Deep learning in transformers**: The transformer architecture deploys a deep learning model that uses layers of self-attention mechanisms. These mechanisms enable the model to weigh the importance of different words in a sentence, providing a nuanced understanding of language context and semantics.

- **Scalability and contextual learning**: With an architecture comprising millions of parameters, these models learn from a vast corpus of text data. They are adept at understanding language patterns, nuances, and even stylistic elements, making them incredibly versatile for various NLP tasks.

Technical sophistication in language applications

When exploring the forefront of artificial intelligence, we look at the capabilities of models such as GPT-3 in language generation and processing alongside the comprehensive training and data requirements that enable these models to understand and generate human-like text, reshaping our interaction with technology.

- **Language generation and processing**: Models such as GPT-3 have demonstrated capabilities in generating coherent and contextually relevant text, responding to natural language prompts, and even performing complex language tasks such as translation, summarization, and question-answering.

- **Training and data requirements**: The training of such models is an extensive process, requiring vast datasets and significant computational resources. The models are fine-tuned on a range of text inputs, from literature and web pages to specific domain texts, ensuring a broad understanding of language and context.

Challenges and considerations in implementation

Implementing generative AI, particularly in enterprise environments such as those facilitated by Dynamics 365 AI, comes with its unique set of challenges and considerations. The journey from concept to deployment of generative AI models involves navigating through technical complexities, ethical implications, and operational integration issues:

- **Data quality, quantity, and bias**: Generative AI models require large volumes of high-quality data to learn and generate accurate, realistic outputs. Ensuring the availability of such datasets, which are free from biases and adequately represent the diversity of real-world scenarios, is a significant challenge. Poor data quality or insufficient datasets can lead to models that generate inaccurate, biased, or even nonsensical outputs.

- **Computational resources**: The training of generative AI models is computationally intensive, requiring significant processing power and memory. Organizations must be prepared to invest in the necessary hardware or cloud-based solutions to support the computational demands of these models. Balancing the cost of these resources against the benefits generative AI can bring to the organization is a critical consideration.

- **Ethical and societal implications**: Generative AI raises important ethical questions, particularly around the authenticity and ownership of generated content. There's also the potential for misuse in creating deceptive or harmful content. Organizations must consider these ethical dimensions and establish guidelines to ensure the responsible use of generative AI. This includes compliance with copyright laws, respect for intellectual property, and mechanisms to prevent the generation of inappropriate or unethical content.

- **Integration with existing systems**: Integrating generative AI models into existing business systems and workflows, such as those managed by Dynamics 365, poses technical and operational challenges. Ensuring that generative AI components can seamlessly interact with other AI models, databases, and applications within the organization's ecosystem requires careful planning and execution.

- **Model training and fine-tuning**: Training generative AI models to produce desired outcomes often involves a process of trial and error, requiring expertise in model architecture and hyperparameter tuning. Additionally, as business needs and data evolve, models must be continually fine-tuned and retrained to maintain their effectiveness and relevance.

- **User trust and acceptance**: Building user trust in the outputs generated by AI is crucial for the successful deployment of generative AI applications. Users need to understand and have confidence in how the AI generates its outputs and the reliability of those outputs in decision-making processes. Fostering this trust requires transparency in AI operations and establishing clear guidelines for use.

- **Monitoring and maintenance**: Ongoing monitoring and maintenance are essential to ensure that generative AI models continue to function as intended over time. This involves regular checks for model drift, updating models with new data, and adjusting to changes in computational infrastructure or data processing pipelines.

In summary, the technical depth and sophistication of generative AI, particularly through GANs and transformer-based models, represent a significant advancement in AI capabilities. As these technologies integrate into Dynamics 365 AI, they open up new possibilities for enhancing business processes, from data generation to complex language understanding and interaction. This deep dive into the technical workings of generative AI sets the stage for comprehending its practical applications and prepares businesses to harness its full potential while understanding the complexities and responsibilities that come with it.

Azure Open AI Service: An in-depth technical exploration

Azure Open AI Service represents a groundbreaking collaboration between Microsoft Azure and OpenAI, providing a powerful platform that combines cutting-edge advancements in AI with robust cloud computing capabilities. This service transcends traditional cloud offerings, ushering in a new era of AI applications in business and technology.

We address how integrating OpenAI's sophisticated AI capabilities with Azure's robust cloud infrastructure provides comprehensive support for model deployment, API integration, and data handling, coupled with dynamic resource management and security measures. This sets the stage for exploring how this fusion of AI and cloud technology is transforming business applications, offering unprecedented scalability, flexibility, and security in AI deployment.

Foundational integration with Microsoft Azure

The Azure OpenAI Service is built on the backbone of Microsoft Azure, leveraging its global network, high-performance computing options, and comprehensive security features. This integration allows Azure to serve as a powerful platform for deploying OpenAI's models, providing users with flexible and scalable AI solutions that can be tailored to a wide range of applications, from natural language processing tasks to complex data analysis.

- **Computing power and scalability**: Azure's computing capabilities are a critical component of this integration, enabling the deployment of OpenAI models at scale. Azure's infrastructure supports a wide array of computing options, including GPU and FPGA-based instances, which are essential for running large AI models efficiently. This allows businesses to scale their AI applications based on demand, ensuring optimal performance and cost-effectiveness.

- **Data privacy and security**: Integrating OpenAI services with Azure brings OpenAI's capabilities into a secure and compliant cloud environment. Azure's comprehensive security features, including network security, encryption, identity and access management, and compliance certifications, ensure that the data processed by OpenAI models is protected according to industry-leading standards. This is particularly crucial for businesses handling sensitive or regulated data.

- **Seamless connectivity and interoperability**: The integration with Azure facilitates seamless connectivity between OpenAI models and Azure services. For instance, Azure's AI and machine learning services, such as Azure Machine Learning, Azure Cognitive Services, and Azure Data

Lake, can easily interact with OpenAI models, enabling a cohesive AI solution where data storage, processing, and advanced AI tasks are tightly integrated.

- **Development and deployment tools**: Azure provides a rich set of tools and services for developing, deploying, and managing AI applications. The Azure OpenAI Service benefits from these tools, offering developers integrated development environments (IDEs), continuous integration and deployment (CI/CD) pipelines, and monitoring and management tools. This ecosystem simplifies the development of AI applications, from experimentation to production.

- **Global reach and local compliance**: By leveraging Azure's global infrastructure, Azure OpenAI Service offers businesses worldwide access to OpenAI's models while adhering to local data residency and compliance requirements. This global reach, combined with local compliance, enables businesses to deploy AI solutions that meet their regulatory obligations across different regions.

By combining the advanced AI capabilities of OpenAI with the robust, enterprise-ready cloud platform of Azure, businesses can accelerate their AI initiatives, driving innovation and achieving competitive advantage in an increasingly AI-driven world.

Operational mechanics of Azure Open AI Service

This section delves into the operational mechanics of Azure OpenAI Service, highlighting how it integrates cutting-edge generative AI capabilities with its robust, scalable infrastructure. This integration not only democratizes access to powerful AI tools but also ensures that organizations can deploy AI solutions with efficiency, security, and compliance at the forefront.

- **Architecture and infrastructure**: At its core, Azure OpenAI Service leverages the cloud-computing infrastructure of Microsoft Azure, providing a secure, scalable platform for deploying OpenAI's advanced models, including the renowned generative pre-trained transformer (GPT) series. The service is built on a modular architecture that allows businesses to integrate generative AI capabilities into their applications through Azure's global network of managed data centers, ensuring low latency and high availability.

- **Deployment and scaling**: The operational mechanics of Azure OpenAI Service are designed for ease of use and scalability. Businesses can deploy OpenAI models as part of their Azure environment, leveraging Azure's computing capabilities to scale their AI applications according to demand. The service supports both batch processing and real-time inference, allowing for flexible integration into a wide range of business processes, from customer service chatbots to content generation and analysis tools.

- **API access and integration**: Azure OpenAI Service provides API access to OpenAI's models, facilitating seamless integration with existing applications and services within the Azure ecosystem. This API-first approach ensures that businesses can easily embed generative AI capabilities into their software solutions without the need for extensive AI expertise. The API supports a variety of programming languages and frameworks, making it accessible to developers with different technical backgrounds.

- **Data privacy and security**: By recognizing the critical importance of data privacy and security, Azure OpenAI Service incorporates Azure's comprehensive security features, including encryption in transit and at rest, role-based access control, and compliance certifications. This ensures that the sensitive data processed by AI models remains secure and that deployments comply with regulatory standards such as GDPR and HIPAA.

- **Customization and fine-tuning**: While Azure OpenAI Service provides access to pre-trained models, it also offers tools for customization and fine-tuning. Businesses can train models on their proprietary data, allowing for the creation of customized AI solutions that are closely aligned with their specific needs and challenges. This fine-tuning process is supported by Azure's AI training and computing resources, enabling efficient model optimization.

- **Monitoring and management**: Azure provides integrated monitoring and management tools for Azure OpenAI Service, allowing businesses to track usage, performance, and costs in real-time. These tools help organizations optimize their AI deployments, ensuring they are running efficiently and cost-effectively. Additionally, Azure's monitoring tools offer insights into model behavior, helping to identify opportunities for improvement and optimization.

- **Community and support**: Azure OpenAI Service benefits from the vast Azure and OpenAI communities, providing businesses with access to a wealth of resources, including documentation, tutorials, and forums. Microsoft Azure also offers enterprise-level support, ensuring that organizations can resolve any issues quickly and maximize their AI investments.

In summary, the operational mechanics of Azure OpenAI Service represent a significant advancement in the deployment and scaling of AI applications. By leveraging the robust infrastructure of Azure and the advanced capabilities of OpenAI's models, businesses can accelerate their AI initiatives, driving innovation and gaining competitive advantages in their respective markets.

Enhancing AI performance in the cloud

Azure OpenAI Service is not just about accessibility to AI; it's about supercharging AI performance in a cloud environment. This portion of the chapter delves into how Azure OpenAI Service amplifies AI capabilities, focusing on performance enhancement, scalability, and integration within the cloud.

- **Optimized AI performance**: Azure OpenAI Service capitalizes on the underlying Azure infrastructure, designed to maximize the efficiency and speed of AI computations. This optimization ensures that even the most complex AI models, such as those developed by OpenAI, run smoothly, with reduced latency and increased throughput. The service leverages Azure's advanced GPUs and CPUs, tailored for AI workloads, to provide the computational power needed to process large datasets and perform intricate model calculations rapidly.

- **Scalability**: One of the critical advantages of deploying AI in the cloud with Azure OpenAI Service is scalability. Organizations can start with minimal resource utilization, suitable for small-scale experiments or applications, and seamlessly scale up their operations to accommodate growing data volumes or more computationally intensive AI models. This flexibility allows businesses to manage costs effectively while ensuring their AI applications can expand in line with their ambitions and needs.

- **Global deployment and accessibility**: Azure OpenAI Service benefits from Azure's global network of data centers, facilitating the deployment of AI applications worldwide with minimal latency. This global reach ensures that AI-driven applications can deliver consistent performance across different regions, enhancing user experience and engagement. Moreover, Azure's comprehensive set of compliance certifications guarantees that AI deployments meet local regulatory requirements, a critical consideration for global enterprises.

- **Integration with the Azure ecosystem**: Enhancing AI performance in the cloud goes beyond raw computational power; it extends into how well the AI services integrate with existing cloud ecosystems. Azure OpenAI Service is deeply integrated with the broader Azure ecosystem, including Azure Data Services, Azure Cognitive Services, and Azure Machine Learning. This integration enables a streamlined workflow where data can be easily ingested, processed, analyzed, and acted upon within the Azure environment, creating a cohesive and efficient AI pipeline.

- **Customization and fine-tuning**: Azure OpenAI Service provides advanced tools for customizing and fine-tuning AI models to specific business requirements. These tools, supported by Azure Machine Learning, allow organizations to adapt pre-trained models by using their datasets and optimizing AI performance for their unique contexts. Fine-tuning AI models in the cloud leverages Azure's computational resources, enabling more accurate and relevant AI outputs without the extensive infrastructure investments traditionally required.

- **Continuous improvement with AI insights**: The service offers robust monitoring and analytics tools, enabling businesses to track AI performance and gain insights into model behavior. These insights can inform continuous improvement cycles, where AI models are regularly updated and optimized based on real-world performance data. This process of iterative enhancement is crucial for maintaining the relevance and effectiveness of AI applications over time.

In conclusion, Azure OpenAI Service represents a significant leap forward in enhancing AI performance in the cloud. By leveraging the power, scalability, and global reach of Azure, alongside deep integration with Azure's ecosystem and advanced customization tools, businesses can unlock unprecedented AI capabilities.

Security, compliance, and ethical considerations

The deployment of AI solutions not only brings about transformative capabilities but also introduces a spectrum of considerations that must be meticulously managed to ensure trust, integrity, and alignment with legal and societal expectations. This segment explores the multifaceted approach required to navigate these aspects within the Azure OpenAI Service ecosystem.

Security measures

Azure OpenAI Service is built upon Microsoft Azure's robust security infrastructure, designed to protect data and operations at every layer. The key security measures include the following:

- **Data encryption**: All data within Azure OpenAI Service, both at rest and in transit, is encrypted using industry-standard protocols. This ensures that sensitive information remains secure from unauthorized access.

- **Access control**: The service implements stringent access controls, including Azure Active Directory (AAD) integration, role-based access control (RBAC), and multifactor authentication (MFA), to ensure that only authorized personnel can access AI resources and data.

- **Network security**: Azure's network security features, such as Azure Firewall and Virtual Networks, provide an additional layer of protection, isolating AI workloads and minimizing exposure to potential threats.

Compliance adherence

Azure OpenAI Service adheres to Microsoft Azure's comprehensive compliance framework, which includes certifications and attestations across global, regional, and industry-specific standards. This compliance framework ensures that AI deployments meet stringent regulatory requirements, including the following:

- **GDPR**: Azure OpenAI Service is designed to support organizations in their compliance with the General Data Protection Regulation (GDPR), offering features for data management, privacy, and governance.

- **HIPAA**: For healthcare organizations, Azure OpenAI Service facilitates compliance with the Health Insurance Portability and Accountability Act (HIPAA), ensuring that patient data is handled with the utmost security and privacy.

Ethical AI use

Beyond security and compliance, the ethical use of AI is a cornerstone of Microsoft's approach. Azure OpenAI Service incorporates several mechanisms to promote ethical AI practices:

- **Fairness and bias mitigation**: Tools and frameworks are available to help developers identify and mitigate biases in AI models, promoting fairness and reducing the risk of unintended discrimination.

- **Transparency and explainability**: Azure OpenAI Service emphasizes the importance of transparency, offering explanations of how AI models make decisions. This is crucial for building trust among users and stakeholders.

- **Responsible AI principles**: Microsoft's commitment to responsible AI is embedded in Azure OpenAI Service, aligning with principles that ensure AI technologies are used to empower and benefit society while avoiding harm.

Operationalizing ethical AI

Implementing Azure OpenAI Service with ethical considerations in mind involves operational practices such as the following:

- **Ethical AI review processes**: Establishing internal review boards or processes to evaluate AI initiatives against ethical principles and guidelines

- **Stakeholder engagement**: Engaging with a broad set of stakeholders, including customers, users, and societal groups, to understand the potential impacts of AI solutions and address concerns proactively

- **Continuous monitoring**: Regularly monitoring AI applications for ethical issues, performance anomalies, and compliance with evolving regulations and standards

In navigating the security, compliance, and ethical landscapes, Azure OpenAI Service offers a robust platform for organizations to leverage powerful AI capabilities while maintaining a commitment to security, legal adherence, and ethical integrity. By prioritizing these considerations, businesses can harness the transformative potential of AI with confidence, ensuring that their innovations contribute positively to their customers, society, and the broader technological ecosystem.

In conclusion, Azure Open AI Service is not just a collaboration between two technology leaders; it's a fusion of advanced AI capabilities with one of the world's most powerful cloud platforms. This service is redefining the possibilities of AI in business, providing an accessible, scalable, and secure environment for leveraging state-of-the-art AI models. As businesses increasingly look to integrate AI into their operations, Azure Open AI Service stands as a testament to what can be achieved when cutting-edge AI meets world-class cloud infrastructure.

Integrating language models and ChatGPT with Dynamics 365 AI

The integration of sophisticated language models, including GPT-3 and ChatGPT, with Dynamics 365 AI marks a significant leap forward in the realm of enterprise software solutions. This section provides an in-depth technical exploration of how these cutting-edge AI tools are seamlessly woven into the Dynamics 365 ecosystem, enhancing its capabilities in customer interaction, data analysis, and overall business intelligence. This integration facilitates seamless data flow and management, enabling the customization and training of AI models to meet specific business needs, thereby revolutionizing customer service, streamlining workflows, and providing advanced analytical insights within the Dynamics 365 ecosystem.

Detailed integration process

- **Systematic embedding**: The integration process begins with embedding the language models into Dynamics 365's infrastructure. This involves establishing a reliable interface where Dynamics 365 applications can interact with the AI models. The embedding is meticulously designed to ensure that the AI models can access necessary data from Dynamics 365 applications without disrupting their core functionalities.

- **API-driven interaction**: Central to this integration is robust API connectivity. Dynamics 365 applications use specific API endpoints to send requests to the AI models and receive responses. These endpoints act as a bridge, translating the business application data into a format that the AI models can process and vice versa.

Architectural foundations of integration

- **Data flow and management**: Managing the flow of data between Dynamics 365 applications and the AI models is a critical aspect. This involves setting up secure, high-throughput channels for data transmission, ensuring latency-free interactions. The architecture is designed to handle large volumes of data, maintaining the integrity and confidentiality of the information being processed.

- **Customization and training of AI models**: Although they were pre-trained on diverse datasets, GPT-3 and ChatGPT often require additional training to adapt to specific business contexts. This customization involves fine-tuning the models with industry-specific data, terminology, and interaction styles, ensuring that the outputs are highly relevant and aligned with the business's unique needs.

Enhancing Dynamics 365 with AI capabilities

- **Revolutionizing customer service**: The integration dramatically transforms customer service modules within Dynamics 365. AI-powered chatbots, equipped with natural language understanding, can interact with customers in a conversational manner, providing instant, accurate, and contextually aware responses to inquiries.

- **Streamlining interaction workflows**: These AI models automate routine customer interactions, such as responding to common queries or providing informational content, thereby freeing up human agents to handle more complex customer needs.

- **Advanced analytical insights**: Beyond customer interaction, the integrated AI models offer profound analytical capabilities. They can sift through vast amounts of textual data within Dynamics 365, extracting key insights, summarizing trends, and predicting future customer behavior, thereby enabling data-driven decision-making.

Addressing implementation challenges

- **Contextual accuracy**: One of the significant challenges is maintaining the accuracy and relevance of AI responses. This is tackled by implementing advanced algorithms that ensure the AI models contextually understand the queries based on the latest business data and customer interaction trends.

- **Data security and privacy**: Integrating these AI models necessitates stringent security protocols. The architecture incorporates encryption, secure data transfer channels, and compliance with international data protection standards to safeguard sensitive information.

- **Optimizing for scalability and performance**: The integration is built to scale and is capable of adjusting to varying levels of demand. Regular performance evaluations and adjustments ensure that the system remains efficient and responsive under different operational loads.

Future enhancements and evolutions

- **Continuous model improvement**: The integration framework is designed for ongoing evolution. As the AI models encounter new data and user interactions, they continuously learn and adapt, improving their accuracy and effectiveness.

- **Expanding application horizons**: When looking ahead, there's potential to broaden the scope of this AI integration across other Dynamics 365 modules, such as finance, operations, and human resources, transforming the suite into a comprehensive, AI-enhanced enterprise solution.

In conclusion, integrating language models and ChatGPT with Dynamics 365 AI represents a fusion of AI innovation with enterprise functionality. This technical deep dive has shown how such integration not only enhances the existing capabilities of Dynamics 365 but also paves the way for more intelligent, automated, and insightful business processes. As we continue to advance in the AI-driven digital era, this integration is poised to be a key differentiator for businesses looking to leverage technology for competitive advantage and operational excellence.

Real-world use cases and implementation examples of integrating language models and ChatGPT with Dynamics 365 AI

The integration of advanced language models and ChatGPT into Dynamics 365 AI is not just a theoretical advancement but a practical revolution in various industries. Here are some real-world use cases and implementation examples that demonstrate the transformative impact of this technology.

Use case 1 – Multinational retail chain enhances customer experience

Background: A leading multinational retail chain faced challenges in managing customer inquiries, especially during peak shopping seasons, leading to customer dissatisfaction.

Implementation:

- The company integrated a GPT-3 powered chatbot with their Dynamics 365 Customer Service module.
- This AI-driven chatbot was trained on extensive customer interaction data, product information, and company policies to ensure accurate and relevant responses.

Functionality:

- The AI chatbot handled a wide array of customer inquiries, from order tracking to product recommendations, with enhanced natural language understanding capabilities.
- Complex queries requiring human input were seamlessly escalated to customer service agents, with the chatbot providing a conversation summary for context.

Real-world impact:

- The retailer saw a drastic improvement in response times and resolution rates, especially during high-demand periods.
- Enhanced customer satisfaction and loyalty were observed, as customers appreciated the personalized and efficient service.
- The company reported significant savings in operational costs and an increase in overall sales revenue.

Use case 2 – Finance consulting firm leverages AI for market analysis

Background: A finance consulting firm sought to provide more dynamic and data-driven investment advice in an unpredictable market.

Implementation:

- They integrated language models with Dynamics 365 Finance, focusing on real-time market analysis and predictive financial modeling.
- The AI system was trained on market trends, historical financial data, and client portfolio profiles for tailored financial insights.

Functionality:

- The AI system provided in-depth analysis of financial reports and market data, offering predictive insights and investment recommendations.

- Advanced algorithms were utilized to automate the generation of financial reports, making complex data understandable for clients.

Real-world impact:

- The firm could offer cutting-edge, AI-enhanced financial analysis, aiding clients in making informed investment decisions.

- Efficiency in report generation and data analysis was significantly improved, allowing analysts to focus on strategic client management.

- The firm established itself as a leader in innovative, AI-driven financial consulting services.

Use case 3 – Global corporation streamlines HR operations

Background: A global corporation aimed to modernize its HR processes to make them more efficient and employee-oriented.

Implementation:

- Integration of ChatGPT with Dynamics 365 Human Resources, with a focus on automated, personalized employee experiences.

- The AI system was trained on the corporation's HR policies and diverse labor laws, and it provided multilingual support.

Functionality:

- The AI system managed initial candidate interactions for recruitment, using advanced language models to assess qualifications.

- For current employees, the system automated responses to HR queries and assisted in routine processes such as leave applications and training registrations.

Real-world impact:

- The recruitment processes were streamlined, with AI efficiently handling initial screenings.

- Employee engagement and satisfaction were enhanced due to prompt and accurate HR responses.

- Significant operational efficiencies were gained in the HR department, allowing a focus on talent development and strategic HR initiatives.

In each instance, the implementation of language models and ChatGPT within Dynamics 365 AI showcases a significant enhancement in operational efficiency and customer/employee satisfaction. These real-world examples underline the potential of AI to revolutionize business processes, offering innovative solutions to traditional challenges in various industry sectors.

Summary

As we draw this chapter to a close, we stand at a pivotal moment in the evolution of business technology. The integration of advanced language models such as GPT-3 and ChatGPT into Dynamics 365 AI is not merely an enhancement of existing capabilities; it is a paradigm shift in how businesses interact with data, engage with customers, and optimize their operations. This chapter has been a journey through the intricate landscape of generative AI, revealing its vast potential and the transformative impact it holds for businesses across various industries.

We delved deep into the technical aspects of embedding generative AI into Dynamics 365, uncovering the nuances of API-driven interactions, data flow management, and the bespoke tailoring of AI models to suit specific business contexts. This technical exploration illuminated the remarkable capabilities of generative AI, from understanding and generating human-like text to offering predictive insights that were once beyond the realm of possibility.

The real-world use cases presented in this chapter—ranging from a multinational retail chain revolutionizing customer service to a financial consulting firm enhancing its analytical prowess—demonstrate the practical applications and tangible benefits of this integration. These scenarios underscored how generative AI could lead to significant improvements in operational efficiency, customer satisfaction, and strategic decision-making. They exemplify the power of AI in transforming customer interactions from transactional exchanges into engaging, personalized experiences and turning vast, unstructured data into valuable business insights.

However, the journey of integrating generative AI into business processes is as challenging as it is exciting. It raises critical questions and considerations regarding data privacy, ethical AI usage, and the mitigation of biases in AI models. As businesses navigate these challenges, the focus must remain on harnessing AI's power responsibly and ethically, ensuring that technological advancement does not outpace the consideration for its broader impact on society.

Looking to the future, the possibilities of what can be achieved with generative AI in Dynamics 365 are limitless. As AI technology continues to advance at a rapid pace, its integration into business applications will likely become more nuanced and sophisticated. Businesses that embrace this technology and adapt to its evolving nature will not only streamline their existing operations but also unlock innovative methods to serve their customers, manage their workforce, and make data-driven decisions.

In closing, this is more than a chapter on technological integration; it is a roadmap for businesses ready to embark on a transformative journey. By embracing the potential of generative AI, organizations can position themselves at the forefront of a new wave of digital innovation, setting new benchmarks in efficiency, customer engagement, and intelligent business practices. As we continue to venture into this AI-augmented era, the insights and lessons from this chapter will undoubtedly serve as valuable guides in navigating the exciting and ever-changing landscape of business technology.

Questions

1. What is the primary function of generative adversarial networks (GANs) in generative AI?

2. How do language models such as GPT-3 enhance Dynamics 365 applications?

3. What role do APIs play in integrating generative AI models with Dynamics 365 AI?

4. Can you describe a real-world application of generative AI in a retail business context with Dynamics 365 AI?

5. What are some of the challenges in integrating generative AI with Dynamics 365 AI?

Answers

1. GANs in generative AI consist of two neural networks, the generator and the discriminator, working in tandem. The generator creates data (such as images, text, etc.) that mimic real-world inputs, while the discriminator evaluates these outputs against actual data. The primary function of GANs is to produce highly realistic and believable outputs by continually refining the generator's capabilities based on the feedback from the discriminator.

2. Language models such as GPT-3 enhance Dynamics 365 applications by providing advanced natural language processing capabilities. They enable these applications to understand and generate human-like text, allowing for more sophisticated customer service chatbots, efficient automation of routine interactions, and insightful data analysis within business contexts.

3. APIs act as a bridge in the integration process, facilitating the communication between Dynamics 365 applications and generative AI models. They allow for the seamless exchange of data, where the AI models receive input from Dynamics 365, process it, and return intelligent responses or analyses. This API-driven interaction is crucial for embedding AI functionalities into business applications effectively.

4. In a retail business context, generative AI can be used to power intelligent chatbots in customer service. When integrated with Dynamics 365 AI, these chatbots can handle a wide range of customer queries in real time, from providing product information to handling order inquiries. This application leads to improved customer service efficiency, quicker response times, and enhanced overall customer satisfaction.

5. The key challenges include ensuring the contextual accuracy and relevance of AI-generated responses, maintaining data privacy and security, and handling the ethical implications of AI deployment. Additionally, businesses must focus on customizing the AI models to fit their specific industry needs and continuously update the models to adapt to changing business environments.

Harnessing MS Copilot for Enhanced Business Insights

In this chapter, we'll embark on an explorative journey into the functionalities and applications of MS Copilot, a revolutionary tool that's redefining the use of technology in business. This chapter aims to unfold the layers of MS Copilot, providing a clear, straightforward understanding of its capabilities and the significant advantages it brings to modern business operations.

We'll begin by introducing MS Copilot, laying out a foundational understanding of what this tool is and the powerful features it possesses. MS Copilot isn't just another piece of technology; it's a sophisticated tool equipped with the capability to analyze complex datasets, make predictions, and offer insights that can guide crucial business decisions. This section aims to demystify the technology behind MS Copilot, making its advanced functionalities accessible and comprehensible.

Then, we'll discuss the seamless integration of MS Copilot with Dynamics 365 AI modules, a crucial aspect for businesses already utilizing Microsoft's platforms. This integration represents a significant stride in enhancing business intelligence and operational efficiency. We'll delve into how MS Copilot complements and elevates the existing capabilities of Dynamics 365, forming a robust system that can process and analyze data more efficiently, thereby enabling businesses to make more informed decisions.

A critical and innovative aspect of MS Copilot is its ability to assist in code generation and optimization. This section is particularly insightful for businesses looking to streamline and enhance their software development processes. We'll explore how MS Copilot not only accelerates these processes but also improves the quality and functionality of software solutions, thereby addressing both efficiency and effectiveness in business operations.

This chapter culminates with a collection of case studies and success stories, illustrating the real-world application and impact of MS Copilot across different industries. These narratives provide a practical perspective, showcasing how various businesses have effectively utilized MS Copilot to enhance their business insights and decision-making processes. From improving operational workflows to achieving better customer engagement, these stories highlight the tangible benefits that MS Copilot can bring to a business.

The following topics will be covered in this chapter:

- Overview of MS Copilot and its comprehensive features

- Integrating MS Copilot with Dynamics 365 AI

- Leveraging MS Copilot for code generation and optimization in Dynamics 365 AI

- Case studies in harnessing MS Copilot for enhanced business insights

In essence, this chapter serves as a comprehensive guide to understanding and utilizing MS Copilot in a business context. It aims to provide both depth and clarity, ensuring that readers from all levels of technical expertise can grasp the potential of MS Copilot. By the end of this chapter, you should have a well-rounded view of how MS Copilot can be a transformative asset for your business operations and strategies in the increasingly data-driven world of business.

Overview of MS Copilot and its comprehensive features

In this section, we'll provide a detailed overview of MS Copilot, a revolutionary product by Microsoft that stands as a testament to the advancements in AI and its applications in business intelligence. MS Copilot is not just an AI tool; it's a comprehensive suite designed to augment various aspects of business operations, from data analysis to customer interaction, while leveraging the latest in machine learning, AI integration, and natural language processing.

Advanced data processing and analysis

At the heart of MS Copilot's capabilities is its advanced data processing and analysis framework, which leverages the power of Microsoft's cloud computing and AI technologies. This section delves into the intricacies of how MS Copilot transforms raw data into actionable insights, facilitating informed decision-making and strategic business planning:

- **Sophisticated data handling**: MS Copilot is engineered to manage and analyze vast amounts of data from diverse sources. It employs state-of-the-art algorithms and machine learning models to sift through data, recognizing patterns, trends, and anomalies that are not immediately apparent. This capability allows businesses to decode complex datasets, uncovering insights that drive growth and efficiency.

- **Real-time data processing**: One of the standout features of MS Copilot is its ability to process data in real-time. This is crucial for businesses operating in fast-paced environments where the ability to make quick, data-driven decisions can be a competitive advantage. Real-time analytics enable organizations to monitor their operations continuously, identify issues as they arise, and capitalize on opportunities at the moment.

- **Deep analytics for predictive insights**: Beyond traditional data analysis, MS Copilot utilizes deep analytics to forecast future trends and behaviors. By applying predictive models to historical data, MS Copilot can provide businesses with forward-looking insights, helping them anticipate market movements, customer behavior changes, and potential operational bottlenecks. This predictive capability supports strategic planning and helps businesses stay ahead of the curve.

- **Natural language processing (NLP) for data interpretation**: MS Copilot incorporates advanced NLP technologies, making it possible to analyze textual data at scale. This includes customer reviews, social media posts, and other forms of unstructured data. By understanding the nuances of human language, MS Copilot can extract sentiment, intent, and qualitative insights, enriching the quantitative analysis with a layer of contextual understanding.

- **Integration with business applications**: A key strength of MS Copilot lies in its seamless integration with other business applications and systems, including Dynamics 365, Microsoft Power Platform, and third-party tools. This interoperability ensures that data analysis is not siloed but deeply embedded in the business processes, enhancing operational workflows, customer relationship management, and enterprise resource planning with data-driven intelligence.

- **Automated reporting and visualization**: To make the insights accessible to decision-makers, MS Copilot features automated reporting and visualization tools. These tools translate complex data analyses into intuitive dashboards and reports, highlighting key metrics, trends, and patterns. Automated reporting not only saves time but also ensures that insights are communicated effectively across the organization, fostering a culture of data literacy.

- **Customizable analysis frameworks**: Recognizing that businesses have unique data analysis needs, MS Copilot offers customizable frameworks. Organizations can tailor the analysis parameters, models, and reporting formats to their specific requirements, ensuring that the insights generated are highly relevant and actionable.

By providing sophisticated data handling, real-time processing, predictive insights, and seamless integration with business applications, MS Copilot empowers organizations to make informed decisions, optimize their operations, and drive strategic initiatives forward in an increasingly data-driven world.

The integration of cutting-edge AI technologies

MS Copilot integration isn't just about harnessing the power of AI; it's about embedding these advanced capabilities deeply within business processes to revolutionize how organizations operate, make decisions, and interact with customers. This section explores the layers and dimensions of how MS Copilot integrates these technologies to offer a comprehensive suite of features:

- **Leveraging advanced machine learning models**: At the heart of MS Copilot's capabilities are the advanced machine learning models that drive its analytics, decision-making, and predictive functionalities. These models are trained on vast datasets, enabling MS Copilot to offer insights that are both deep and wide-ranging. From predicting customer behavior to optimizing supply chain logistics, these machine learning models are finely tuned to enhance business operations and strategic planning.

- **NLP**: MS Copilot integrates sophisticated NLP technologies to interpret, understand, and generate human-like text. This allows businesses to automate customer service inquiries, extract valuable insights from unstructured data such as customer feedback, and even generate content that resonates with human readers. NLP capabilities in MS Copilot enable businesses to communicate more effectively, both internally and with their customers, breaking down barriers and opening new avenues for engagement.

- **Computer vision for enhanced interaction**: Through the integration of computer vision, MS Copilot can analyze and interpret visual data, adding another layer of intelligence to business applications. From processing images in customer support tickets to automating inventory checks through visual feeds, computer vision expands the scope of what's possible with AI, making MS Copilot a more versatile tool for businesses across various sectors.

- **Autonomous systems and robotics integration**: MS Copilot's capabilities extend into the realm of autonomous systems and robotics, offering potential applications in manufacturing, logistics, and even customer interactions. By integrating AI-driven autonomous technologies, MS Copilot can streamline operations, enhance efficiency, and open up new possibilities for automation that were previously beyond reach.

- **Conversational AI for seamless interactions**: The integration of conversational AI technologies within MS Copilot enables the creation of sophisticated chatbots and virtual assistants. These AI-driven entities can handle a wide range of tasks, from addressing customer inquiries to assisting with internal operations, all in a manner that feels natural and human-like. This not only enhances customer satisfaction but also frees up human resources to focus on more complex tasks.

- **AI ethics and governance**: Recognizing the importance of responsible AI use, MS Copilot incorporates ethical AI frameworks and governance models. This ensures that AI technologies are used in a manner that is transparent, fair, and accountable. By embedding ethical considerations into the fabric of its AI integrations, MS Copilot helps organizations navigate the complex landscape of AI ethics, ensuring that their use of AI aligns with societal values and regulatory requirements.

- **Seamless integration with Microsoft's ecosystem**: A key aspect of MS Copilot's strength lies in its seamless integration with the broader Microsoft ecosystem, including Azure cloud services, Dynamics 365 applications, and Microsoft 365 productivity tools. This interconnectedness allows businesses to leverage AI across all facets of their operations, from backend processes to customer-facing applications, all within a unified and secure environment.

In conclusion, the integration of cutting-edge AI technologies within MS Copilot represents a significant leap forward for business intelligence and operational automation. By harnessing advanced machine learning, NLP, computer vision, and conversational AI, among others, MS Copilot empowers businesses to achieve new levels of efficiency, innovation, and customer engagement. As AI technologies continue to evolve, MS Copilot remains at the cutting edge, ensuring that businesses have access to the most advanced tools available to drive their success in the digital age.

Enhancing business intelligence

MS Copilot incorporates a suite of advanced AI capabilities that significantly enhance data analysis, insight generation, and decision-making processes. This transformation enables businesses to navigate complex market dynamics with agility and precision. Here's an in-depth exploration of how MS Copilot is setting new standards for enhancing business intelligence:

- **Real-time data analysis and reporting**: MS Copilot revolutionizes business intelligence through its real-time data analysis capabilities. Leveraging Azure's powerful computing infrastructure, MS Copilot processes vast amounts of data from diverse sources almost instantaneously. This real-time processing allows businesses to receive up-to-the-minute insights, enabling rapid response to emerging trends, operational issues, or customer behavior changes. Moreover, MS Copilot's sophisticated reporting tools automate the generation of insightful, easy-to-interpret reports, significantly reducing the time and effort traditionally required for business intelligence reporting.

- **Predictive analytics and forecasting**: At the forefront of MS Copilot's business intelligence enhancement features are its predictive analytics and forecasting capabilities. Utilizing machine learning models, MS Copilot analyzes historical data patterns to predict future trends, customer demands, and potential market shifts. This foresight allows businesses to proactively adjust their strategies, optimize operations, and mitigate risks before they materialize, ensuring they remain competitive and resilient in volatile markets.

- **Customizable dashboards and visualizations**: MS Copilot provides customizable dashboards and data visualization tools that present complex data sets in an intuitive and accessible manner. Businesses can tailor these dashboards to highlight **key performance indicators** (**KPIs**) that are relevant to their specific operational goals and strategies. By transforming data into visual formats, such as charts and graphs, MS Copilot enables stakeholders at all levels to quickly understand business metrics, fostering a data-driven culture within the organization.

- **Advanced analytics with NLP**: Integrating advanced NLP capabilities, MS Copilot takes business intelligence a step further by enabling users to query data using natural language. This means that business users can obtain insights by asking questions in plain English, without the need for complex query languages. NLP also powers sentiment analysis, allowing businesses to gauge customer sentiments from social media, customer reviews, and feedback, providing a more nuanced understanding of the customer experience.

- **Seamless integration with business ecosystems**: MS Copilot's strength lies in its seamless integration with the broader Microsoft ecosystem and third-party applications. This integration ensures that data flows freely across systems, breaking down silos and providing a holistic view of the business. By connecting data from Dynamics 365, Microsoft 365, third-party CRMs, ERPs, and other data sources, MS Copilot enables comprehensive business intelligence that spans all functional areas of the organization.

- **AI-driven decision support**: Beyond analytics and reporting, MS Copilot serves as an AI-driven decision support system, offering recommendations and actionable insights. By analyzing data patterns and business outcomes, MS Copilot can suggest strategies for improving customer engagement, operational efficiency, and financial performance. These AI-generated recommendations are based on data-driven analysis, ensuring that business decisions are grounded in solid insights.

- **Ethical AI and governance**: Acknowledging the critical importance of ethical considerations and governance in AI, MS Copilot incorporates mechanisms to ensure the responsible use of AI technologies. This includes data privacy controls, bias detection and mitigation, and compliance with regulatory standards. By prioritizing ethical AI, MS Copilot not only enhances business intelligence but also ensures that AI applications align with corporate values and societal norms.

In conclusion, MS Copilot is redefining business intelligence by harnessing the power of AI to offer real-time insights, predictive analytics, customizable dashboards, and advanced analytics capabilities. Its integration within the Microsoft ecosystem and commitment to ethical AI further solidify its role as a transformative tool for businesses aiming to harness data for strategic advantage. With MS Copilot, organizations are equipped to navigate the complexities of today's business environment with confidence and foresight.

User experience and interface design

This section explores how MS Copilot's user experience and interface design stand out, making advanced technology seamlessly usable for everyday business tasks:

- **Intuitive interaction models**: MS Copilot's interface is designed around intuitive interaction models that facilitate natural, conversational engagements with the system. Leveraging the latest in NLP and conversational AI, it enables users to query data, request analyses, and even execute tasks through simple, natural language commands. This reduces the learning curve and makes advanced AI functionalities accessible to users without requiring them to understand complex query languages or navigate through intricate menus.

- **Adaptive interface design**: The interface of MS Copilot is adaptive, dynamically adjusting to fit the context of the user's task and the device being used. Whether accessing Copilot on a desktop for deep analytics work or a mobile device for quick status checks and approvals, the interface presents the information and controls most relevant to the task at hand. This responsive design ensures that users have a consistent and efficient experience across all platforms.

- **Visualization and dashboard customization**: A key feature of MS Copilot is its powerful visualization tools, which transform complex datasets into clear, actionable insights through graphs, charts, and interactive dashboards. These visual representations are not only customizable but also designed with best practices in data visualization in mind to ensure they communicate information effectively. Users can personalize dashboards to highlight the metrics most relevant to their roles and preferences, enhancing the decision-making process with visually intuitive data storytelling.

- **Accessibility and inclusivity**: MS Copilot's interface design is rooted in principles of accessibility and inclusivity, ensuring that users with varied abilities can navigate and utilize the system effectively. This includes adherence to web accessibility standards, which includes offering options for text size, contrast settings, and support for screen readers. By prioritizing accessibility, MS Copilot democratizes access to AI-driven insights and functionalities, embodying Microsoft's commitment to empowering every individual and organization.

- **Feedback-driven iteration**: The development of MS Copilot's user interface is an ongoing, iterative process driven by user feedback. This approach ensures that the system evolves in ways that directly address the needs and challenges of its users. Regular updates to the interface reflect this commitment to improvement, incorporating new features and refinements that enhance usability and satisfaction.

- **Seamless integration with Microsoft's ecosystem**: MS Copilot's interface design benefits from seamless integration with the broader Microsoft ecosystem, including Microsoft 365 and Dynamics 365. This integration provides a familiar look and feel for users already accustomed to Microsoft products, fostering a cohesive user experience across applications. Additionally, it allows Copilot functionalities to be embedded directly within other Microsoft applications, streamlining workflows and reducing the need to switch between different tools.

- **Guidance and support**: Recognizing the potential complexity of navigating AI-driven systems, MS Copilot includes built-in guidance and support features directly within the interface. Interactive tutorials, contextual help, and AI-powered suggestions aid users in leveraging the system's capabilities, providing on-the-spot assistance to enhance learning and adoption.

In essence, the user experience and interface design of MS Copilot embody a thoughtful approach to making advanced AI and analytics both powerful and accessible. By focusing on intuitive design, personalization, and seamless integration, MS Copilot ensures that users can harness the full potential of AI to drive business insights and decisions, all within an interface that is engaging, efficient, and inclusive:

- **Intuitive design**: MS Copilot boasts a user-friendly interface that makes navigating complex AI functionalities straightforward for users of all technical backgrounds

- **Flexible customization**: The platform offers extensive customization options, allowing it to adapt to the specific needs and preferences of different businesses

Real-time interaction and automated customer support

MS Copilot enhances real-time interaction and automates customer support, thereby transforming the customer experience and operational efficiency:

- **Real-time interaction capabilities**: MS Copilot leverages cutting-edge AI to enable real-time interactions with customers across various platforms. Whether through chatbots on a website, messaging apps, or voice assistants, MS Copilot provides customers with immediate responses to their inquiries. This capability is underpinned by advanced NLP algorithms, which allow the system to understand and interpret customer queries accurately, engaging in conversations that feel natural and human-like.

- **Automated customer support**: One of the key strengths of MS Copilot is its ability to automate customer support processes. By integrating with Microsoft's Azure Bot Service and other AI models, MS Copilot can handle a wide range of customer support tasks, from answering frequently asked questions to troubleshooting common issues. This automation extends to more complex inquiries as well, where MS Copilot can guide customers through detailed processes, gather necessary information, and even perform tasks such as booking appointments or processing returns.

- **Personalization in customer interactions**: MS Copilot takes customer interaction a step further by personalizing the customer support experience. Utilizing data analytics and machine learning, MS Copilot can tailor conversations to the specific needs and history of each customer. This personalized approach not only enhances customer satisfaction but also increases the efficiency of support interactions by directly addressing the customer's unique situation and preferences.

- **Seamless handoff to human agents**: Recognizing the limitations of AI in handling every customer support scenario, MS Copilot is designed to facilitate a seamless handoff to human agents when necessary. This ensures that customers are always provided with the support they need, even when their inquiries require a personal touch or exceed the AI's capabilities. The handoff process is smooth, with MS Copilot providing the human agent with all the relevant context and information that was gathered during the initial interaction, thereby ensuring a cohesive customer experience.

- **Integration with CRM and ERP systems**: MS Copilot's effectiveness in automating customer support is further enhanced by its deep integration with **customer relationship management** (**CRM**) and **enterprise resource planning** (**ERP**) systems. This integration allows MS Copilot to access and update customer records in real time, ensuring that all interactions are logged and that customer information is always current. Additionally, by leveraging data from these systems, MS Copilot can provide more informed and context-aware support.

- **Continuous learning and improvement**: MS Copilot's AI models are designed for continuous learning, which means that with every interaction, the system becomes more adept at understanding customer queries and providing accurate support. This self-improving mechanism ensures that the quality of automated customer support continually enhances over time, reflecting the changing needs and behaviors of customers.

- **Enhancing customer support with AI insights**: Beyond direct customer interactions, MS Copilot utilizes AI-driven insights to improve the overall customer support strategy. By analyzing interaction data, MS Copilot can identify trends, common issues, and areas for improvement. These insights empower businesses to make data-driven decisions about their customer support processes, optimizing them for better efficiency and customer satisfaction.

By leveraging AI to provide immediate, personalized, and efficient support, MS Copilot not only improves the customer experience but also significantly enhances operational efficiency, setting a new standard for customer service in the digital age.

In conclusion, MS Copilot represents a significant stride in the realm of business technology, combining advanced AI capabilities with user-centric design and functionality. As businesses navigate an increasingly data-driven and competitive landscape, MS Copilot stands as a crucial ally, offering a range of tools and features that drive efficiency, enhance customer engagement, and foster intelligent decision-making. This comprehensive overview sets the stage for a deeper exploration of MS Copilot's specific applications in subsequent sections, showcasing its potential to revolutionize various aspects of modern business operations.

Integrating MS Copilot with Dynamics 365 AI

In the contemporary digital era, the integration of MS Copilot with Dynamics 365 AI modules emerges as a transformative development in business technology. This strategic fusion heralds a new age of AI-driven solutions, combining the advanced AI of MS Copilot with the comprehensive business functionalities of Dynamics 365. This section embarks on an in-depth exploration of this integration, dissecting how it revolutionizes the domain of business applications, enhances operational processes, and pioneers innovative AI strategies. It aims to provide a holistic understanding of the integration's multifaceted impact, from technical enhancements to strategic business implications.

Harmonizing advanced technologies

- **Technical fusion and system harmonization**: The core of this integration lies in the sophisticated fusion of MS Copilot's AI prowess with Dynamics 365's extensive business capabilities. This involves a meticulous process of aligning data structures, system algorithms, and operational workflows, ensuring a seamless and efficient integration of the two platforms. The harmonization of these advanced technologies is key to unlocking their combined potential and enhancing system functionality and operational efficiency.

- **Seamless data integration and management**: A significant aspect of this integration is the seamless management and synchronization of data between MS Copilot and Dynamics 365. This process ensures that data flows effectively between the platforms, facilitating real-time analytics and decision-making while maintaining data integrity and security.

Enhancing Dynamics 365 with AI

- **Revolutionizing code development processes**: This integration brings a paradigm shift in code development within Dynamics 365. MS Copilot introduces automated, optimized coding processes, significantly improving efficiency and reducing the margin for error. This advanced approach to coding accelerates the development life cycle of Dynamics 365 applications, paving the way for more sophisticated and robust software solutions.

- **Elevating AI functionalities and analytics**: The addition of MS Copilot's AI features to Dynamics 365 transforms its capabilities, introducing enhanced analytics, predictive modeling, and intelligent automation. This integration allows businesses to delve deeper into data analytics, offering more nuanced insights and fostering data-driven decision-making.

Best practices and real-world integration scenarios

- **Showcasing diverse applications across industries**: Various industries, from finance to healthcare, have experienced transformative impacts from integrating MS Copilot with Dynamics 365. These real-world examples illustrate the integration's broad scope and versatility, demonstrating how it leads to enhanced decision-making, customer engagement, and operational efficiencies.

- **Strategies for effective integration**: This section provides comprehensive insights into best practices for integrating MS Copilot with Dynamics 365. It covers strategic considerations for a successful implementation, including navigating potential challenges and maximizing the integration's benefits for business operations.

Transforming business operations and development

- **Streamlining project development and implementation**: The synergy between MS Copilot and Dynamics 365 redefines traditional development workflows. It fosters more agile, efficient, and innovative approaches to project implementation, enabling businesses to respond swiftly to evolving market demands and customer needs.

- **Encouraging a culture of innovation and creativity**: Beyond enhancing operational processes, this integration instills a culture of innovation and creative problem-solving in development teams. It encourages developers to explore new methodologies and innovative solutions, fostering an environment where creativity and technological advancement go hand in hand.

In conclusion, the integration of MS Copilot with Dynamics 365 AI modules marks a pivotal moment in the field of business technology. This comprehensive exploration has provided an extensive overview of how this integration can optimize coding processes, enrich AI functionalities, and transform development workflows, setting new benchmarks in AI-driven business applications. As the business landscape continues to evolve in the digital age, this powerful combination of MS Copilot and Dynamics 365 emerges as a crucial strategy for businesses seeking to harness advanced technology for operational excellence, enhanced efficiency, and innovative solutions in a competitive market.

Leveraging MS Copilot for code generation and optimization in Dynamics 365 AI

The integration of MS Copilot with Dynamics 365 AI is reshaping the landscape of software development. This detailed exploration focuses on the technical aspects of how MS Copilot facilitates enhanced code generation and optimizes development processes within the Dynamics 365 AI ecosystem. It delves into the sophisticated AI-driven capabilities of MS Copilot, including intelligent code suggestions, auto-completion, and automated code generation, providing developers with in-depth knowledge and strategies to write high-quality code more efficiently, accelerate development timelines, and maximize the potential of Dynamics 365 AI for comprehensive business insights:

- **Deep dive into intelligent code suggestions**: MS Copilot's code suggestion feature is based on complex machine learning algorithms that analyze vast repositories of coding data. This section examines how these algorithms process patterns in code structure, syntax, and usage to offer contextually relevant, accurate coding suggestions. It explores the underlying AI technology, including NLP and predictive analytics, enabling MS Copilot to understand the developer's intent and offer suggestions that align with the specific architecture and coding practices of Dynamics 365 AI.

- **Enhancing productivity with auto-completion**: MS Copilot's auto-completion tool is engineered to significantly expedite the coding process. This part of the chapter provides a technical analysis of how MS Copilot's AI models anticipate a developer's next lines of code based on the current coding context and historical data trends. It also discusses how this feature ensures consistency in coding standards and adherence to the best practices in Dynamics 365 AI development, thus maintaining code quality across projects.

- **Automated code generation and its algorithms**: The automated code generation capability of MS Copilot is a testament to its advanced AI and machine learning foundations. This segment delves into the sophisticated algorithms that enable MS Copilot to write functional blocks of code autonomously. It covers the technical workings of these algorithms, discussing how they can recognize patterns, extract key functions, and generate optimized, bug-resistant code that integrates seamlessly with Dynamics 365 AI modules.

- **Strategies for optimizing the development workflow**: Successfully integrating MS Copilot into existing development workflows involves strategic planning and a deep understanding of both MS Copilot and Dynamics 365 AI. This section offers a technical guide on how to blend MS Copilot's features into development processes effectively. It discusses methods to integrate intelligent suggestions and automated code into the development life cycle, enhancing the efficiency and quality of Dynamics 365 AI applications.

- **Case studies – real-world technical implementations**: To illustrate the practical applications of these technologies, this part presents detailed case studies where MS Copilot has been effectively used in Dynamics 365 AI development. These cases delve into specific technical challenges and solutions, showcasing how MS Copilot's capabilities have been leveraged to optimize coding processes and enhance AI-driven functionalities in diverse business scenarios.

- **Maximizing Dynamics 365 AI for business insights**: The ultimate goal of integrating MS Copilot in Dynamics 365 AI development is to unlock the platform's full potential in delivering insightful business intelligence. This section emphasizes the technical benefits of enhanced coding practices, such as increased application reliability, scalability, and performance. It highlights how these improvements enable businesses to leverage their Dynamics 365 AI applications for deeper analytics, more personalized customer interactions, and data-driven decision-making.

In conclusion, leveraging MS Copilot for code generation and optimization in Dynamics 365 AI is a pivotal development in software engineering. This comprehensive section has provided a technical deep dive into how MS Copilot transforms coding processes, enriching AI-driven functionalities and boosting overall development efficiency. As businesses progress in a technology-centric world, the integration of advanced tools such as MS Copilot in Dynamics 365 AI development is essential for gaining a competitive advantage and harnessing the full power of AI for innovative and insightful business solutions.

Case studies in harnessing MS Copilot for enhanced business insights

The integration of MS Copilot into business processes has demonstrated transformative effects across various industries. This section delves into detailed case studies, showcasing how different organizations have successfully harnessed MS Copilot to achieve enhanced business insights and operational efficiencies. Each case study is a narrative that combines technical sophistication with practical business applications, offering a comprehensive view of MS Copilot's capabilities.

Case study 1 – revolutionizing retail with personalized customer experiences

Background: A multinational retail chain, ShopMax, was facing challenges in personalizing shopping experiences and managing a complex inventory across its global outlets.

Implementation: ShopMax integrated MS Copilot into their Dynamics 365 AI system, focusing on customer data analysis for personalized marketing and inventory optimization using predictive analytics.

Technical approach: Utilizing MS Copilot's NLP capabilities, ShopMax developed a system that analyzed customer feedback and shopping patterns to create personalized product recommendations. Additionally, MS Copilot's predictive models helped forecast inventory needs, reducing waste and overstock.

Outcome: The implementation resulted in a 35% increase in customer engagement and a 40% reduction in inventory mismanagement. ShopMax's targeted marketing campaigns, powered by personalized insights, significantly increased customer loyalty and sales.

Case study 2 – enhancing healthcare services with predictive analytics

Background: HealthFirst, a healthcare provider, struggled with managing patient influx and resource allocation.

Implementation: HealthFirst utilized MS Copilot to develop an AI-driven system within Dynamics 365 that predicted patient admission rates and optimized resource management.

Technical approach: By analyzing historical patient data and current health trends, MS Copilot provided accurate predictions of patient admissions. It also optimized staff scheduling and resource allocation based on these predictions.

Outcome: The predictive system improved patient care efficiency by 25% and resource utilization by 20%. HealthFirst saw a notable decrease in patient wait times and a significant improvement in overall patient satisfaction.

Case study 3 – streamlining manufacturing with AI-driven supply chain optimization

Background: AutoBuild, a car manufacturer, needed to enhance its supply chain and production efficiency.

Implementation: AutoBuild adopted MS Copilot to create a sophisticated supply chain management system within their Dynamics 365 framework.

Technical approach: MS Copilot analyzed production data, supply chain logistics, and market demand to create an optimized manufacturing workflow. It identified bottlenecks and predicted supply needs, preventing production delays.

Outcome: AutoBuild experienced a 30% improvement in supply chain efficiency and a 15% increase in production speed, leading to higher customer satisfaction and reduced operational costs.

Case study 4 – financial services' strategic decision-making with market analytics

Background: SecureInvest, a financial services firm, aimed to improve its investment strategies and advisory services.

Implementation: SecureInvest leveraged MS Copilot to enhance its Dynamics 365 AI system, focusing on market trend analysis and personalized financial advice.

Technical approach: Using MS Copilot's data processing and machine learning algorithms, SecureInvest developed a tool that analyzed market trends, predicted investment risks, and offered personalized portfolio recommendations for clients.

Outcome: The firm achieved a 20% increase in investment performance and client satisfaction. Its data-driven investment strategies and personalized advisory services significantly attracted more clients and enhanced customer trust.

These case studies provide insightful examples of how MS Copilot, when integrated effectively with business systems such as Dynamics 365, can lead to substantial improvements in customer experiences, operational efficiency, and strategic decision-making. Each story is a testament to MS Copilot's ability to transform data into actionable insights, driving businesses toward greater success in a competitive landscape.

Summary

As we conclude this chapter, we recognize the profound transformation that MS Copilot has brought to the Dynamics 365 AI environment. This journey has not only highlighted the capabilities and adaptability of MS Copilot but also underscored its pivotal role in revolutionizing business processes and decision-making across various industries.

The integration of MS Copilot into Dynamics 365 AI has demonstrated a seamless melding of cutting-edge AI with sophisticated business processes. This powerful combination enhances every facet of business operations, from the way we approach code generation to the intricacies of implementing predictive analytics and automating customer interactions. MS Copilot emerges not just as a tool but as a driver of innovation, steering businesses toward more efficient, precise, and intelligent operational models.

Through in-depth case studies covering the retail, healthcare, manufacturing, and financial sectors, we have seen tangible evidence of MS Copilot's impact. These stories illustrate how effectively harnessed AI can lead to significant improvements in efficiency, customer engagement, and strategic insight. Each case study serves as a practical example, providing valuable lessons and insights into integrating AI into business strategies and operations.

One of the most significant revelations of this chapter is the empowerment that MS Copilot offers businesses in terms of enhanced insights. By leveraging the platform's advanced capabilities, organizations can delve deeper into analytics, tailor customer experiences more effectively, optimize operations, and make more data-driven decisions. This empowerment is crucial in today's data-centric business world, where leveraging such insights is key to maintaining a competitive advantage and driving growth.

Looking ahead, the integration of advanced AI tools, such as MS Copilot, into business systems such as Dynamics 365 AI is becoming increasingly essential in our rapidly evolving digital world. The insights from this chapter not only pave the way for future innovations but also inspire businesses to embrace AI-driven solutions. They challenge current approaches to problem-solving, customer engagement, and operational efficiency, highlighting the need for continuous adaptation and learning in the face of technological advancements.

The importance of embracing a culture of continuous learning and adaptation was a recurring theme in this chapter. As AI technologies evolve, businesses must adapt their strategies and approaches to stay abreast of these changes. Embracing advancements, integrating new tools effectively, and learning from real-world applications are crucial steps for any business looking to succeed in the technology-driven future.

In summary, this chapter provided a comprehensive overview of how integrating MS Copilot with Dynamics 365 AI can revolutionize business operations. It brought together insights and experiences demonstrating the potential of MS Copilot to enhance business processes, enrich AI functionalities, and transform development workflows, setting a new benchmark in AI-driven business applications. As we step into a future where digital transformation is paramount, the integration of MS Copilot in Dynamics 365 AI stands as a key strategy for businesses seeking to harness the power of AI for innovative, efficient, and insightful solutions.

The next chapter will address the use of virtual agents for customer service in the context of MS Copilot and Microsoft Dynamics.

Questions

1. What key feature of MS Copilot has revolutionized code generation in Dynamics 365 AI, and how does it benefit the development process?

2. How has the integration of MS Copilot impacted the retail industry, based on the case studies discussed in this chapter?

3. What role does MS Copilot play in enhancing the AI functionalities of Dynamics 365 applications?

4. Can you describe how MS Copilot contributes to making informed business decisions in the financial services sector?

5. What is the significance of continuous learning and adaptation when integrating MS Copilot into business operations?

Answers

1. MS Copilot's key feature that has revolutionized code generation is its AI-driven capabilities for automating complex coding tasks and providing intelligent code suggestions. This feature benefits the development process by reducing the time and effort required for coding, improving accuracy, and ensuring adherence to best coding practices.

2. In the retail industry, the integration of MS Copilot with Dynamics 365 AI has led to significant improvements in personalizing customer experiences and managing inventory. The AI-driven insights from MS Copilot enabled the development of personalized marketing strategies and more efficient inventory management, leading to increased customer engagement and reduced overstock.

3. MS Copilot enhances the AI functionalities of Dynamics 365 applications by introducing advanced features such as predictive analytics, intelligent data processing, and machine learning models. This allows businesses to gain deeper insights, optimize business processes, and create more personalized customer interactions.

4. In the financial services sector, MS Copilot contributes to making informed business decisions by analyzing market trends and customer portfolios to provide data-driven investment strategies and personalized financial advice. This leads to improved investment performance, higher customer satisfaction, and better portfolio management.

5. Continuous learning and adaptation are crucial when integrating MS Copilot into business operations because AI technologies constantly evolve. Businesses need to stay updated with these advancements, adapt their strategies, and learn from real-world applications to effectively utilize MS Copilot to enhance their operations and maintain a competitive edge in the market.

"Virtual Agent for Customer Service" in the Context of MS Copilot and Microsoft Dynamics

In the contemporary landscape of customer service, the advent of virtual agents, particularly within the ecosystem of MS Copilot and Microsoft Dynamics, is setting a new standard in customer engagement and support. This chapter delves deep into this cutting-edge technology, spotlighting its transformative role when integrated with Microsoft's renowned business solutions.

At the outset, the chapter presents an in-depth analysis of how virtual agents, powered by MS Copilot, are being implemented for automated customer support. These agents represent a synergy of advanced AI technology with the practicalities of customer service. Their deployment in environments powered by Microsoft Dynamics products is a game-changer. With capabilities honed by **machine learning (ML)** and **natural language processing (NLP)**, these virtual agents are not just automating routine customer interactions but are also providing sophisticated, context-aware responses to complex queries. This section elucidates how these AI-driven agents enhance efficiency, provide 24/7 support, and elevate the standard of customer interactions to new heights.

Moving forward, the chapter shifts focus to the construction and refinement of conversational AI interfaces and chatbots within the MS Copilot and Microsoft Dynamics framework. It details the technological underpinnings that enable these virtual agents to conduct interactions that are indistinguishable from human ones. The intricacies involved in crafting these responsive systems – from their initial design to the continuous refinement of their conversational abilities – are examined. This part of the chapter underscores the importance of creating virtual agents that are not only technically proficient but also capable of delivering a seamless and engaging customer experience.

The integration of these virtual agents into customer service processes within Dynamics 365 forms a crucial part of the discussion. This segment offers a granular view of how virtual agents can be seamlessly incorporated into existing Dynamics 365 infrastructures, enhancing and complementing the customer service capabilities of these systems. It discusses the challenges and innovative strategies involved in embedding these AI solutions into established customer service workflows, ensuring they work in unison with human agents to provide a comprehensive customer service experience.

Concluding with a series of practical case studies, the chapter brings theoretical concepts to life. These real-world examples from various industries demonstrate the successful implementation and significant impact of virtual agents within Dynamics 365-driven environments. The case studies highlight improved response times, enhanced customer satisfaction, and cost efficiencies, providing valuable insights and strategies for organizations looking to embark on similar implementations.

In essence, *Virtual Agent for Customer Service* offers a thorough exploration of MS Copilot's virtual agents within the Microsoft Dynamics ecosystem. It provides a detailed understanding of their technical capabilities, practical implementation strategies, and their potential to revolutionize customer service. For businesses leveraging Microsoft Dynamics products, this chapter serves as an essential guide to harnessing the power of AI-driven virtual agents to transform their customer service operations and achieve impactful business outcomes.

Here is a list of topics covered:

- Implementing virtual agents for automated customer support with MS Copilot
- Integration of virtual agents with customer service processes in Dynamics 365
- Case studies and success stories in virtual agent implementation

Implementing virtual agents for automated customer support with MS Copilot

As businesses strive to innovate in customer service, the implementation of virtual agents, especially those powered by MS Copilot, is becoming increasingly pivotal. This section provides a comprehensive examination of how virtual agents are revolutionizing customer support, detailing their technological foundations, integration processes, functionalities, and best practices for effective implementation.

Implementing Microsoft Copilot as a virtual agent involves integrating it with your existing customer service infrastructure. This could be a website, a mobile app, or a **customer relationship management (CRM)** system such as Microsoft Dynamics. Once integrated, Microsoft Copilot can start handling customer queries, freeing up your human agents to focus on more complex tasks.

Step 1: Understanding your customer service infrastructure

Before implementing Microsoft Copilot, it's crucial to understand your existing customer service infrastructure. This could be a website, a mobile app, or a CRM system such as Microsoft Dynamics. Understanding the current setup will help you identify the best way to integrate Microsoft Copilot.

Step 2: Integration with existing infrastructure

Once you have a clear understanding of your existing infrastructure, the next step is to integrate Microsoft Copilot. This involves setting up the necessary **application programming interfaces (APIs)** and ensuring that Microsoft Copilot can access the data it needs to function effectively. For instance, if you're using Microsoft Dynamics, you'll need to ensure that Microsoft Copilot can access customer data, order history, and other relevant information.

Step 3: Customizing Microsoft Copilot

Microsoft Copilot comes with a range of features that can be customized to suit your business needs. For example, you can customize the language and tone of Microsoft Copilot to match your brand voice. You can also train Microsoft Copilot on your specific business domain, enabling it to provide more accurate and relevant responses to customer queries.

Step 4: Testing and iteration

After integrating and customizing Microsoft Copilot, it's important to thoroughly test it before rolling it out to customers. This involves running a series of tests to ensure that Microsoft Copilot is correctly interpreting and responding to customer queries. Based on the results of these tests, you may need to make further adjustments to Microsoft Copilot's settings or training data.

Step 5: Deployment and monitoring

Once testing is complete, you can deploy Microsoft Copilot to start handling customer queries. However, the work doesn't stop there. It's important to continuously monitor Microsoft Copilot's performance and make adjustments as needed. This will ensure that Microsoft Copilot continues to provide high-quality customer service.

Implementing Microsoft Copilot as a virtual agent involves a careful process of integration, customization, testing, and continuous improvement. By following these steps, businesses can leverage Microsoft Copilot to provide automated, efficient, and high-quality customer service.

Advanced technological infrastructure of virtual agents

Virtual agents such as Microsoft Copilot are powered by a sophisticated technological infrastructure that enables them to provide intelligent, automated customer support. Here's a detailed look at the key components of this infrastructure:

- **Continuous learning and evolution**: At the heart of every virtual agent is an AI engine that uses ML algorithms to understand and respond to customer queries. These algorithms are trained on large datasets, enabling the virtual agent to learn from past interactions and continually improve its performance.

- **AI-driven interaction capabilities**: Virtual agents in MS Copilot are embedded with sophisticated AI algorithms that enable nuanced understanding and interaction, closely resembling human conversation. These agents leverage a blend of advanced ML, NLP, and data analysis technologies, including tasks such as sentiment analysis, which allows the virtual agent to gauge the customer's mood and respond appropriately, and entity recognition, which helps the virtual agent identify key pieces of information in the customer's query.

- **Integration of APIs with current and future systems**: Virtual agents need to be integrated with the business's existing customer service infrastructure. This is achieved through APIs, which allow the virtual agent to access necessary data and functions. For instance, if the virtual agent is integrated with a CRM system, it can use APIs to retrieve customer data, order history, and other relevant information.

- **Cloud computing for scalable and reliable service**: Virtual agents often leverage cloud computing to deliver scalable, reliable, and cost-effective service. With cloud computing, businesses can easily scale up their virtual agent infrastructure to handle increased customer queries during peak times. The cloud also provides robust data storage and processing capabilities, enabling the virtual agent to handle complex tasks and large volumes of data.

- **Security and privacy**: Given the sensitive nature of customer data, virtual agents must have robust security and privacy measures in place. This includes data encryption, secure APIs, and compliance with data protection regulations. Businesses must also ensure that their virtual agent infrastructure provides transparency and control over how customer data is used.

In conclusion, the advanced technological infrastructure of virtual agents enables them to provide intelligent, personalized, and efficient customer service. As technology continues to evolve, we can expect virtual agents to become even more sophisticated and capable.

Seamless integration with customer support systems

Customer service has evolved beyond traditional call centers. Today, businesses are leveraging AI-powered virtual agents to provide automated customer support. One such advanced AI is Microsoft Copilot, which serves as a virtual agent for customer service, capable of understanding and responding to customer queries in real time. This section provides a detailed, step-by-step guide to seamlessly integrating a virtual agent such as Microsoft Copilot with your customer support systems.

Step 1: Understand your existing infrastructure

Before you can integrate a virtual agent, you need to understand your existing customer support infrastructure. This could be a website, a mobile app, a CRM system such as Microsoft Dynamics, or even a social media platform. The virtual agent needs to be able to interact with these systems to access necessary data and provide effective customer support.

Step 2: *Choose the right virtual agent*

Choose a virtual agent that best suits your business needs. Microsoft Copilot, for instance, is a versatile and powerful virtual agent that can be customized to match your brand voice and understand specific business terminologies.

Step 3: *Set up API integration*

APIs are the backbone of seamless integration. They allow the virtual agent to communicate with your existing customer support systems. You'll need to set up these APIs to allow the virtual agent to retrieve necessary data and perform actions as needed.

Step 4: *Customize the virtual agent*

Once the APIs are set up, you can customize the virtual agent to fit your business needs. This could involve configuring the virtual agent to understand specific business terminologies, or customizing its responses to align with your company's brand voice.

Step 5: *Test the integration*

After setting up and customizing the virtual agent, you should thoroughly test the integration. This involves running a series of tests to ensure that the virtual agent is correctly interpreting and responding to customer queries.

Step 6: *Deploy and monitor*

Once testing is complete, you can deploy the virtual agent to start handling customer queries. However, it's important to continuously monitor the virtual agent's performance and make adjustments as needed. This will ensure that the virtual agent continues to provide high-quality customer service.

Remember – integrating a virtual agent is not a one-time process. As your business evolves, so too should your virtual agent. Continuous learning and improvement are key to maintaining an effective virtual agent.

The seamless integration with customer support systems is a key feature of virtual agents such as Microsoft Copilot. It allows them to provide effective, personalized customer support, enhancing the customer experience and boosting business efficiency. This step-by-step guide provides a roadmap for businesses looking to leverage the power of virtual agents for their customer service needs.

Diverse capabilities and functionalities

Microsoft Copilot is revolutionizing the way businesses interact with their customers. These AI-powered assistants are equipped with a wide range of capabilities and functionalities that make them an invaluable tool for any business:

- **Multilingual support**: One of the key capabilities of Microsoft Copilot is its ability to understand and communicate in multiple languages. This allows businesses to provide customer support in the language that their customers are most comfortable with, enhancing the customer experience.

- **Real-time assistance**: Microsoft Copilot can provide real-time assistance to customers, answering their queries quickly and efficiently. This reduces wait times for customers and allows businesses to handle a larger volume of queries without the need for additional human resources.

- **Error identification and rectification**: Microsoft Copilot is capable of identifying errors in a conversation and rectifying them by offering accurate information. This ensures that customers always receive the most up-to-date and correct information.

- **Understanding images**: In addition to text-based interactions, Microsoft Copilot can also understand images that the user uploads. This extends its capabilities beyond traditional chatbots and allows it to provide more comprehensive support.

- **Generating creative content**: Microsoft Copilot can generate imaginative and innovative content such as poems, stories, code, essays, songs, and more. This makes it a versatile tool that can be used for a wide range of tasks beyond customer support.

- **Integration with existing systems**: Microsoft Copilot can be seamlessly integrated with existing customer support systems, allowing businesses to leverage its capabilities without disrupting their existing workflows.

The diverse capabilities and functionalities of virtual agents such as Microsoft Copilot make them a powerful tool for businesses. Whether it's providing multilingual support, offering real-time assistance, understanding images, or generating creative content, Microsoft Copilot is equipped to handle a wide range of tasks, making it an invaluable asset for any business.

Enhancing operational efficiency and customer experience

Virtual agents such as Microsoft Copilot are transforming the way businesses operate, leading to enhanced operational efficiency and improved customer experience. Here's how:

- **Streamlining customer support**: Microsoft Copilot can handle a large volume of customer queries simultaneously, providing immediate, real-time assistance. This reduces the workload on human agents, allowing them to focus on more complex tasks that require human intervention. As a result, businesses can streamline their customer support operations, leading to increased efficiency.

- **24/7 availability**: Unlike human agents, Microsoft Copilot is available 24/7. This means that customers can get support whenever they need it, regardless of time zones or business hours. This not only enhances the customer experience but also allows businesses to cater to a global customer base.

- **Personalized customer experience**: Microsoft Copilot can be customized to match the brand voice, creating a more personalized experience for customers. It can also be trained on specific business domains, enabling it to provide more accurate and relevant responses to customer queries. This level of personalization can significantly enhance the customer experience.

- **Data-driven insights**: Microsoft Copilot can collect and analyze data from customer interactions, providing valuable insights into customer behavior and preferences. These insights can be used to further improve the customer experience and inform business decisions.

- **Cost efficiency**: By automating routine tasks and handling large volumes of queries, Microsoft Copilot can help businesses reduce their operational costs. This makes it a cost-effective solution for businesses of all sizes.

Microsoft Copilot can significantly enhance operational efficiency and improve the customer experience. Its 24/7 availability, personalization capabilities, data-driven insights, and cost efficiency make it a powerful tool for any business looking to optimize its operations and deliver superior customer service.

Implementation best practices

- **Tailored customization and training**: For maximum effectiveness, it's crucial to customize virtual agents according to specific business contexts and train them with relevant datasets, including industry-specific knowledge and company policies

- **Incorporating customer feedback loops**: Implementing mechanisms for customers to provide feedback on their interactions with virtual agents is essential for continuous improvement and relevance

- **Clear human escalation protocols**: Establishing protocols for seamlessly escalating complex issues to human agents ensures that customers receive comprehensive support, balancing automated efficiency with a human touch

Ongoing monitoring and enhancement

- **Analyzing performance metrics**: Regularly assessing virtual agents' performance through metrics such as response accuracy and customer satisfaction ratings is vital for gauging their effectiveness

- **Continuous updates and adjustments**: Keeping virtual agents updated with the latest advancements in AI technology and adjusting their operational parameters based on performance analytics ensures their sustained effectiveness

In conclusion, the implementation of virtual agents for automated customer support, particularly through MS Copilot, marks a transformative step in customer service strategy. These AI-driven agents not only streamline operational efficiency and elevate the customer experience but also represent a proactive approach to embracing technological advancements in customer engagement. As this technology matures, it is set to become a fundamental component of customer service, redefining standards for responsiveness, personalization, and efficiency in the business world.

In conclusion, the construction of conversational AI interfaces and chatbot capabilities within the MS Copilot and Microsoft Dynamics frameworks is a strategic endeavor that significantly enhances customer interaction. These advanced chatbot solutions not only improve customer engagement but also streamline the customer support process, making it more efficient and effective. As these technologies continue to evolve, they offer immense potential for businesses to innovate in their approach to customer service.

Integration of virtual agents with customer service processes in Dynamics 365

Integrating virtual agents into Dynamics 365's customer service processes is a transformative step for businesses aiming to elevate their customer support systems. This detailed exploration focuses on the intricate process of embedding AI-driven virtual agents into the Dynamics 365 ecosystem, covering the complex technicalities, strategic implementation approaches, and the comprehensive benefits of this integration.

Business considerations for effective deployment

Implementing virtual agents with customer service processes in Dynamics 365 can bring significant benefits to a business, but it also requires careful consideration. Here are some key business considerations:

- **Cost implications**: While virtual agents can reduce the need for human customer service representatives, there are costs associated with their implementation and maintenance. These include the cost of the virtual agent platform, integration costs, and ongoing costs for training and updates.

- **Data security and privacy**: Virtual agents have access to sensitive customer data. Businesses must ensure that they comply with all relevant data protection regulations. This includes securing customer data and providing transparency about how customer data is used.

- **Customer acceptance**: Not all customers may be comfortable interacting with a virtual agent. Businesses should consider their customer demographics and preferences when deciding to implement a virtual agent.

- **Integration with existing systems**: The virtual agent needs to be seamlessly integrated with existing customer service systems. This requires technical expertise and may involve updating or modifying existing systems.

- **Training and updates**: Virtual agents require ongoing training and updates to ensure they continue to provide accurate and relevant responses. This requires a commitment of time and resources.

- **Performance monitoring**: Businesses need to regularly monitor the performance of the virtual agent to ensure it is effectively resolving customer queries. This may require the implementation of new performance metrics and monitoring systems.

While virtual agents can enhance customer service processes, businesses need to carefully consider these factors to ensure a successful implementation.

Strategic approaches for effective integration

- **Leveraging data for personalized interactions**: Virtual agents utilize the rich customer data available in Dynamics 365, including past interactions, purchasing history, and customer preferences. This data-driven approach enables the agents to provide highly personalized customer service experiences.

- **Automating routine customer service tasks**: Virtual agents are programmed to handle and automate various routine tasks in the customer service workflow, such as initiating service tickets, categorizing customer inquiries, and responding to common questions, which enhances the overall efficiency of the process.

Advanced customer interaction and support capabilities

- **Handling multiple forms of customer interactions**: These virtual agents are designed to manage diverse types of customer interactions, ranging from text- and chat-based communications to more complex voice interactions, offering flexibility and convenience to customers.

- **Streamlining query resolution process**: By taking over a substantial volume of routine customer inquiries, virtual agents significantly reduce the workload on human agents. This enables the human customer service team to focus on addressing more complex, sensitive, or high-value customer interactions.

Focused training and customization for optimal functionality

- **Targeted training with Dynamics 365 data**: Virtual agents are extensively trained using actual customer interaction data sourced from Dynamics 365. This specialized training is crucial for equipping the agents with the ability to accurately comprehend and respond to customer queries in a manner that aligns with the business's specific needs and practices.

- **Adaptive learning for continuous improvement**: Designed with adaptive learning capabilities, these virtual agents evolve their performance based on continuous interaction data, ensuring that their service quality improves consistently.

Addressing challenges in integration

- **Upholding data privacy and security standards**: The integration process prioritizes the privacy and security of customer data. Implementing stringent data protection measures and secure API connections is vital to maintain customer trust and comply with data security regulations.

- **Harmonizing AI with human customer service**: Establishing an effective balance between automated responses by virtual agents and the empathetic touch of human agents is key. The integration includes setting up clear protocols for smoothly transitioning complex or sensitive issues to human representatives when necessary.

Evaluating impact and effectiveness

- **Comprehensive performance analysis**: Post-integration, evaluating the performance of virtual agents through detailed metrics such as customer query resolution time, customer satisfaction ratings, and overall impact on customer service efficiency is crucial for assessing their effectiveness

- **Iterative feedback for refinement**: Regularly collecting and analyzing feedback from both customers and human service agents provides valuable insights for continuously refining and enhancing virtual agents' functionalities and responses

Overall, the integration of virtual agents into Dynamics 365's customer service processes represents a significant leap in harnessing AI for improving customer support. This approach not only streamlines operations but also significantly enhances the quality of customer interaction, positioning businesses at the forefront of innovative and efficient customer service in today's digital era.

Case studies and success stories in virtual agent implementation

The following case studies provide examples of how the features addressed in this chapter can be leveraged for real-world applications.

Case study 1 – Retail giant enhances customer experience with AI virtual agents

Background: A leading global retail chain faced challenges managing customer inquiries, especially during high-traffic seasons such as holidays, leading to long wait times and diminished customer satisfaction.

Implementation:

The company implemented virtual agents powered by MS Copilot within their Dynamics 365 customer service system.

These virtual agents were designed to handle a wide range of customer inquiries, from tracking orders to handling returns and exchanges.

Outcomes:

- **Improved response times**: The virtual agents significantly reduced response times. Customers received instant replies to common queries, which previously took minutes or even hours.

- **Increased customer satisfaction**: Customers expressed higher satisfaction due to the quick and accurate responses provided by the virtual agents.

- **Reduced support costs**: The reduction in routine inquiry handling by human agents led to a decrease in overall customer support costs.

- **Key insight**: This implementation showcased how virtual agents could handle high volumes of routine inquiries efficiently, freeing human agents to deal with more complex issues and thus enhancing overall customer service quality.

Case study 2 – Financial services firm boosts efficiency with AI virtual agents

Background: A multinational financial services company struggled with the high volume of customer queries regarding account information, transaction details, and general financial advice, leading to extended wait times.

Implementation:

The firm integrated AI virtual agents into its existing Dynamics 365 customer service platform.

These agents were programmed to handle financial inquiries, provide account updates, and even offer basic financial advice.

Outcomes:

- **Streamlined query resolution**: The virtual agents efficiently resolved common queries, leading to a more streamlined customer service process

- **Enhanced customer experience**: Customers benefited from immediate, 24/7 support for their routine financial inquiries

- **Operational cost savings**: The firm observed a noticeable reduction in operational costs related to customer support

- **Key insight**: This case study demonstrates the effectiveness of virtual agents in handling specialized queries in the financial sector, proving that even industries with complex customer inquiries can benefit significantly from AI integration

Case study 3 – Healthcare provider improves patient support with virtual agents

Background: A large healthcare provider was overwhelmed with patient inquiries regarding appointment scheduling, medical records, and general health questions, leading to long wait times and patient dissatisfaction.

Implementation:

The provider implemented MS Copilot-powered virtual agents within their customer service operations.

These agents were equipped to handle appointment bookings, provide information on medical records, and answer general health-related queries.

Outcomes:

- **Reduced wait times for patients**: Patients experienced significantly reduced wait times for their inquiries

- **Improved patient satisfaction**: The immediate and accurate responses from the virtual agents led to increased patient satisfaction levels

- **Cost efficiency in patient support**: The healthcare provider saw a reduction in the costs associated with patient support services

- **Key insight**: This implementation highlights the potential of virtual agents in the healthcare industry, not only improving operational efficiency but also enhancing the patient support experience

These case studies exemplify the transformative impact of virtual agents within customer service operations across various industries. They demonstrate that virtual agents can significantly improve response times, increase customer satisfaction, and reduce support costs, providing valuable insights and strategies for businesses looking to implement similar AI-driven solutions.

Summary

As we conclude the chapter, it becomes clear that the integration of advanced virtual agents represents a significant evolution in customer service technology. The journey through this chapter has provided a comprehensive overview of the transformative impact these AI-driven solutions have on customer support, particularly within the MS Copilot and Microsoft Dynamics ecosystems.

The chapter began with an exploration of the implementation of virtual agents for automated customer support. It highlighted how these AI-driven solutions enhance operational efficiency and responsiveness in handling customer inquiries. This integration streamlines the customer service process, allowing human agents to concentrate on more complex and nuanced customer needs, thereby optimizing overall workflow and efficiency.

Delving into the development of conversational AI interfaces and chatbots, the chapter emphasized the crucial role of advanced NLP technologies. These technologies are instrumental in creating engaging, responsive, and effective customer interactions. The process of designing these AI systems to be intuitive and capable of handling diverse customer needs was outlined, demonstrating how they provide a personalized and satisfying experience for customers through human-like conversations.

The integration of virtual agents within Dynamics 365's customer service processes was another focal point of the chapter. This section detailed strategic and technical considerations necessary for successful integration, ensuring that AI solutions effectively complement human customer service capabilities. The ability of virtual agents to access and utilize customer data within Dynamics 365 to offer tailored support significantly enhances the customer experience.

Finally, the chapter presented a series of case studies and success stories from various industries. These real-world examples showcased the benefits of virtual agent implementations, such as improved response times, increased customer satisfaction, and enhanced operational efficiency. These stories served as practical demonstrations of the effective utilization of virtual agents, providing valuable insights for businesses planning to adopt these technologies.

In summary, this chapter has offered a thorough exploration of next-generation customer service technologies. The integration of virtual agents into customer service operations presents a compelling opportunity for businesses to elevate their customer support systems. As we advance in the digital era, the strategies and insights provided in this chapter will be invaluable for organizations aiming to leverage AI to enhance their customer service experiences.

Questions

1. How do virtual agents powered by MS Copilot and integrated with Microsoft Dynamics enhance automated customer support?

2. What role do advanced NLP technologies play in the development of conversational AI interfaces and chatbots?

3. Describe the importance of integrating virtual agents with Dynamics 365's customer service processes.

4. What are some of the key benefits highlighted in the case studies and success stories of virtual agent implementation?

5. In what ways do virtual agents continuously improve their performance and relevance in customer service?

Answers

1. Virtual agents in MS Copilot, integrated with Microsoft Dynamics, enhance automated customer support by handling routine inquiries efficiently, providing 24/7 support, and allowing human agents to focus on more complex tasks. They leverage customer data from Dynamics 365 to offer personalized support and streamline the overall customer service process.

2. Advanced NLP technologies enable conversational AI interfaces and chatbots to understand, process, and respond to customer queries in a manner that is both contextually relevant and empathetic. NLP is essential for creating engaging and effective customer interactions that mimic human-like conversations.

3. Integrating virtual agents with Dynamics 365's customer service processes is crucial for ensuring seamless access to customer data, which allows virtual agents to provide tailored support. This integration ensures a cohesive operation where AI solutions complement human customer service efforts, enhancing the overall quality of service.

4. The case studies and success stories in the chapter highlight key benefits of virtual agent implementation, such as significant improvements in response times, increased customer satisfaction, and operational cost savings. These benefits demonstrate the practical impact and effectiveness of virtual agents in diverse industry settings.

5. Virtual agents continuously improve their performance and relevance by learning from ongoing customer interactions and feedback. They use this data to refine their responses, adapt to changing customer needs, and enhance their conversational abilities, ensuring that their service quality improves over time.

10
Fraud Protection with Dynamics 365 AI

In an era where digital transactions and interactions form the backbone of most business operations, the threat of fraud looms larger than ever. Against this backdrop, Dynamics 365 AI stands as a beacon of innovation, offering a suite of AI-driven tools designed to safeguard businesses from the pervasive risks of fraudulent activities. This chapter is dedicated to unraveling the layers of artificial intelligence technology that Dynamics 365 AI harnesses to fortify business operations against fraud. It aims to provide a comprehensive overview of the strategies, tools, and methodologies that organizations can leverage to protect their financial and reputational integrity.

At the core of Dynamics 365's AI approach to fraud protection is its sophisticated machine-learning algorithms and advanced analytics. These technologies dive deep into the ocean of transactional and operational data, identifying subtle anomalies, suspicious patterns, and aberrant behaviors indicative of potential fraud. This chapter will dissect the architecture of fraud detection algorithms, offering readers an intricate understanding of how these systems detect, analyze, and neutralize threats before they can inflict damage.

Beyond the theoretical exploration of AI technologies, this chapter emphasizes the practical application of Dynamics 365 AI in crafting a robust fraud protection framework. It details the process of integrating state-of-the-art fraud detection models directly into the Dynamics 365 ecosystem, focusing on the nuances of monitoring transactions in real time and establishing automated workflows for alerts and risk mitigation. Through practical guidance, readers will learn how to adeptly configure these AI-driven systems to create a proactive defense mechanism against fraud.

To bridge theory with practice, this chapter will also present a collection of case studies and success stories, illustrating how diverse organizations have successfully implemented Dynamics 365 AI to combat fraud. These real-world examples will showcase the transformative impact of AI in enhancing security measures, reducing financial losses, and bolstering business trust. Readers will gain insights into effective fraud protection strategies and learn from the experiences of organizations that have navigated the challenges of implementing AI-driven fraud protection measures.

Here is a list of topics covered in this chapter:

- AI-driven fraud detection and prevention strategies
- Identifying anomalies and patterns using advanced analytics
- Leveraging Dynamics 365 AI for real-time fraud monitoring and mitigation
- Case studies and success stories in fraud protection insights

By navigating the contents of this chapter, you will embark on a detailed exploration of AI's role in fraud protection, equipped with the knowledge to harness Dynamics 365 AI for their fraud defense needs. By the end, the goal is to demystify the use of AI in safeguarding business operations and to provide a clear, actionable framework for employing Dynamics 365 AI's cutting-edge tools for fraud detection and prevention. By adopting these advanced technologies, businesses can not only enhance their ability to detect and prevent fraud but also build a resilient, secure, and operational ecosystem that upholds stakeholder confidence and maintains customer trust.

AI-driven fraud detection and prevention strategies

The application of AI in fraud detection within Dynamics 365 AI embodies a multifaceted approach, combining the nuanced capabilities of **machine learning (ML)**, **natural language processing (NLP)**, and predictive analytics to create a robust defense against fraudulent activities. Let's explore these components in more detail and how they integrate into fraud prevention strategies.

Machine learning for pattern recognition

Pattern recognition involves identifying and classifying patterns in data. In the context of machine learning, these patterns could be anything from visual patterns in images, patterns in time-series data, or patterns in customer behavior.

- **Supervised learning**: These ML models are trained on labeled datasets, learning to distinguish between fraudulent and legitimate transactions based on historical examples. This training enables the models to apply learned patterns to new transactions, effectively predicting potential fraud.

  Let's consider an example of supervised learning for pattern recognition in the context of credit card fraud detection:

  Problem: Credit card fraud detection

  In this scenario, the goal is to classify credit card transactions as either "fraudulent" or "legitimate" based on various transaction attributes:

  I.   **Data collection**: The first step is to collect a dataset of credit card transactions that have already been labeled as "fraudulent" or "legitimate." This dataset will be used to train and test the machine learning model.

II.   **Feature extraction**: Next, we need to convert the raw transaction data into a format that the machine learning algorithm can understand. This is known as feature extraction. In this case, we might use transaction attributes such as transaction amount, time of transaction, location, and other behavioral patterns.

III.   **Model training**: Now we're ready to train our model. We might choose a machine learning algorithm such as logistic regression, decision trees, or neural networks for this task. During training, the model learns to associate patterns in the transaction data with the "fraudulent" or "legitimate" labels.

IV.   **Model evaluation**: After the model has been trained, we need to evaluate its performance. This typically involves using a separate testing dataset to see how well the model can classify new transactions it hasn't seen before.

V.   **Prediction**: Once we're satisfied with the model's performance, we can use it to classify new transactions as they occur. If the model detects patterns in a transaction that it associates with fraud, it can automatically flag that transaction for further investigation.

This is a simplified example, but it illustrates the basic process of using supervised learning for pattern recognition in fraud detection. The key idea is that the model learns to recognize patterns in the data that are associated with specific labels.

- **Unsupervised learning**: In contrast, unsupervised learning algorithms analyze unlabeled data, identifying anomalies or outliers in transaction patterns that might indicate fraudulent activity. This is particularly useful for detecting novel or evolving fraud tactics that have not been previously identified.

Let's use the same example of unsupervised learning for pattern recognition in the context of credit card fraud detection.

Problem: Credit card fraud detection

In this scenario, the goal is to identify unusual or suspicious patterns in credit card transactions that could indicate fraudulent activity:

I.   **Data collection**: The first step is to collect a dataset of credit card transactions. Unlike supervised learning, this data doesn't need to be labeled as "fraudulent" or "legitimate."

II.   **Feature extraction**: Next, we need to convert the raw transaction data into a format that the machine learning algorithm can understand. This is known as feature extraction. In this case, we might use transaction attributes such as transaction amount, time of transaction, location, and other behavioral patterns.

III.   **Model training**: Now, we're ready to train our model. We might choose an unsupervised learning algorithm such as K-means clustering or DBSCAN for this task. During training, the model learns to identify clusters or groups in the data. These clusters represent patterns of normal behavior.

IV.   **Anomaly detection**: After the model has been trained, it can be used for anomaly detection. This involves identifying transactions that don't fit into any of the normal behavior clusters. These anomalies could potentially represent fraudulent transactions.

V.   **Investigation and confirmation**: Once potential fraud cases have been identified, they can be flagged for further investigation. This might involve contacting the cardholder to confirm whether the transaction was legitimate or not.

This illustrates the basic process of using unsupervised learning for pattern recognition in fraud detection. The key idea is that the model learns to recognize patterns of normal behavior, and anything that deviates from these patterns is considered suspicious.

Natural language processing for fraudulent claims detection

In the context of fraudulent claims detection, NLP can be used to analyze the textual data associated with a claim to identify patterns or anomalies that might suggest fraudulent activity. Here's a step-by-step explanation of how this process works:

1.   **Data collection**: The first step is to collect the textual data associated with a claim. This could include the claim description, customer communication, and any other relevant text data.

2.   **Text preprocessing**: Next, the text data is preprocessed to prepare it for analysis. This involves cleaning the data (removing irrelevant information such as stop words and punctuation), normalizing the data (converting all text to lowercase, for example), and tokenizing the data (breaking the text down into individual words or tokens).

3.   **Feature extraction**: Once the text data is preprocessed, features are extracted from the data. This might involve creating a "bag of words" model, where each unique word in the text is considered a feature, or it might involve more complex techniques such as term frequency-inverse document frequency (TF-IDF) or word embeddings.

4.   **Model training**: After the features are extracted, a machine learning model is trained on the data. The model learns to associate certain patterns in the text data with fraudulent or non-fraudulent claims.

5.   **Prediction**: Once the model is trained, it can be used to analyze new claims. The text data associated with a new claim is preprocessed, and the features are extracted. Then, the model predicts whether the claim is likely to be fraudulent based on the patterns it has learned.

6.   **Evaluation**: Finally, the model's predictions are evaluated for accuracy. If the model's performance is not satisfactory, the model may be retrained or the feature extraction process may be adjusted.

In conclusion, NLP can be a powerful tool for fraudulent claims detection, allowing businesses to analyze and learn from the textual data associated with a claim. However, it's important to note that NLP should be used as part of a broader fraud detection strategy and not relied upon as the sole method of detecting fraud.

Predictive analytics for future threat identification

Predictive analytics is a branch of advanced analytics that uses historical data, statistical algorithms, and machine learning techniques to identify the likelihood of future outcomes. In the context of future threat identification, predictive analytics can be used to forecast potential security threats or fraudulent activities:

- **Risk scoring**: Risk scoring is a process that assigns a numerical value, or score, to a specific threat based on its perceived level of risk. This score is typically calculated based on a variety of factors, including the potential impact of the threat, the likelihood of it occurring, and the vulnerability of the system or data it could affect. When combined with predictive analytics, risk scoring can help prioritize threats, allowing organizations to focus their resources on addressing the most significant risks first. For example, a predictive model might identify a number of potential threats and risk scoring might then be used to prioritize these threats based on their risk scores.

- **Trend analysis**: Trend analysis involves analyzing current and historical data to identify patterns or trends. In the context of threat identification, trend analysis can help identify new or emerging threats, as well as changes in the frequency or severity of existing threats. When used alongside predictive analytics and risk scoring, trend analysis can provide additional context that can help improve the accuracy of threat predictions. For example, if trend analysis identifies an increasing number of a particular type of security incident, this information can be used to adjust the risk scores for this type of threat or to train predictive models to better recognize this type of threat.

Predictive analytics, risk scoring, and trend analysis can work together to enhance future threat identification. By combining these techniques, organizations can more accurately predict, prioritize, and respond to potential threats.

Continuous learning and adaptation

A critical advantage of AI-driven strategies in Dynamics 365 AI is the ability to continuously learn and adapt. Machine learning models are regularly updated with new data, allowing them to refine their detection capabilities and stay ahead of evolving fraud schemes.

Integration challenges and considerations

While the potential of AI in fraud detection is immense, organizations face challenges in integrating these advanced technologies into their existing systems. Key considerations include data privacy concerns, the need for substantial training data to develop accurate models, and the ongoing requirement to update and maintain AI systems to adapt to new fraud tactics.

In essence, leveraging AI-driven fraud detection and prevention strategies within Dynamics 365 AI offers a comprehensive and dynamic approach to safeguarding organizational assets. By continuously evolving with new data and trends, Dynamics 365 AI empowers organizations to stay one step ahead of fraudsters, ensuring financial stability and maintaining customer trust in an increasingly digital world.

Identifying anomalies and patterns using advanced analytics

The cornerstone of effective fraud detection in the digital age lies in the ability to identify anomalies and patterns that signify potential fraudulent activity. Dynamics 365 AI harnesses the power of advanced analytics, leveraging a myriad of data points and sophisticated algorithms to illuminate these indicators. This detailed examination explores the multifaceted approach to anomaly detection and pattern recognition, emphasizing how Dynamics 365 AI integrates these capabilities to preempt and combat fraud.

Sophisticated data analysis tools and techniques

Advanced analytics in Dynamics 365 AI encompasses a broad spectrum of data analysis techniques and tools designed to dissect and interpret complex datasets. This includes the following:

- **Descriptive analytics**.
- **Comprehensive visibility and performance metrics**: When using Microsoft Copilot for Service, you gain access to a comprehensive set of analytics. These analytics reveal key performance indicators (KPIs) specific to your Copilot for Service instance. Multiple charts depict trends and usage patterns related to your Copilot's topics, all enhanced with AI insights. These topics are critical; they have the greatest impact on your Copilot's overall performance.
- **Navigating the analytics page**: After publishing your Copilot, you can check essential performance metrics. The analytics section is divided into several pages, offering multiple ways to understand your Copilot's performance. To access these analytics, navigate to the **Analytics** page within Copilot for Service.

  Key terms used on the **Analytics** page include the following:

  - **Conversation**: An ongoing interaction between a specific user or group of users and your Copilot.
  - **Analytics Sessions**: These track user engagement with your Copilot, capturing how well it handles user tasks.
  - **Transcripts**: Conversation transcripts are usually available for download after an analytic session ends. They provide insights into interactions and outcomes.

Extending with Copilot Studio

If you extend Copilot for Service with the custom dialogs (topics) created in Copilot Studio, additional analytics apply. Sessions become engaged when non-system topics are triggered. Engaged sessions can have outcomes such as "resolved" or "abandoned." The Copilot marks a session as resolved when it successfully redirects to the "End of Conversation" topic or lets the session time out.

This foundational layer of analytics provides a snapshot of historical data, outlining baseline behaviors and transaction patterns. Dynamics 365 AI utilizes descriptive analytics to establish normative data profiles against which anomalies can be detected.

Diagnostic analytics

Diagnostic analytics plays a pivotal role. It's the art of dissecting data, identifying anomalies, and diagnosing underlying issues.

Diagnostic analytics provides a magnifying glass for Copilot performance. It helps uncover bottlenecks, inefficiencies, and unexpected behaviors. When your Copilot stumbles, diagnostic analytics steps to diagnose the ailment.

Key features include the following:

- **Conversation insights**: Dive into individual interactions between users and Copilot by identifying patterns of confusion, frequent fallbacks, or unexpected response
- **Session health metrics**: Monitor the overall health of Copilot sessions by detecting session timeouts, unresolved queries, or exceptional behavior
- **Transcripts and interaction flow**: Analyze conversation transcripts and trace the flow of interactions by understanding where Copilot veered off course or excelled

Going a step further, diagnostic analytics investigates the causes behind observed behaviors. Through techniques such as drill-down, data discovery, and correlations, Dynamics 365 AI can uncover underlying factors indicative of fraud.

Traditionally, statistical models have underpinned processes such as inventory management, production planning, and forecasting. However, the industry has reached a plateau in terms of algorithmic improvements. AI emerged as a formidable ally, specifically in **supply chain management** (**SCM**).

Dynamics 365 supply chain management's advanced AI-powered demand forecasting

In the dynamic landscape of supply chain management, accurate demand forecasting is a critical success factor. Dynamics 365 supply chain management seamlessly incorporates advanced AI techniques into its demand planning process:

- **AI-infused demand forecasting models**
  - The system taps into the potential of built-in out-of-the-box AI-powered algorithms
  - It integrates existing models and utilizes the capabilities of custom Azure machine learning (AML).

- These models enhance the precision of demand planning by analyzing historical data, identifying patterns, and projecting future demand with a high degree of accuracy

- **Outlier detection and seasonality analysis**

  - Dynamics 365 supply chain management employs robust techniques to identify outliers and anomalies

  - Seasonality analysis helps account for recurring patterns, such as seasonal demand fluctuations

  - By considering these factors, the system refines its forecasts and adapts to changing conditions.

- **Scenario planning**

  - The solution allows for scenario-based demand planning

  - Users can simulate different scenarios (e.g., market changes and supply disruptions) and assess their impact on demand

  - This capability enables proactive decision-making and risk mitigation

Microsoft Intune Advanced Analytics

Microsoft Intune Advanced Analytics provides comprehensive visibility of the end-user experience in your organization and optimizes it with data-driven insights. Here's how it enhances IT operations:

- **Custom device scopes**: Slices endpoint analytics reports based on scope tags to focus on specific subsets of enrolled devices

- **Anomalies monitoring**: Proactively detects and resolves endpoint issues following configuration changes

- **Enhanced device timeline**: Accesses more events and lower data latency for efficient troubleshooting

- **Device query**: Get near-real-time access to device state and configuration data

- **Battery health report**: Gain visibility into hardware performance issues impacting user experience

Machine learning for enhanced detection

Machine learning models offer a dynamic approach to identifying fraud-related anomalies and patterns:

- **Deep learning**: A subset of machine learning, deep learning models, especially neural networks, are adept at processing vast amounts of unstructured data, such as text and images. Dynamics 365 AI can leverage deep learning to analyze transactional documents and customer correspondences for signs of forgery or deceit.

- **Decision Trees and Random Forests**: These models are particularly useful for classification tasks in fraud detection. By breaking down data into smaller subsets and making decisions at each node, Dynamics 365 AI can classify transactions as fraudulent or legitimate with high accuracy.

Real-time analytics for immediate action

The effectiveness of Dynamics 365 AI in fraud detection critically relies on its real-time analytics capabilities. Without continuous, real-time data analysis, the risk of detecting threats too late escalates. Therefore, the need for immediate analysis, coupled with well-defined fraud triggers, is pivotal in preventing issues as they emerge in real time:

- **Streaming analytics**: This allows Dynamics 365 AI to process and analyze data in real time as it streams into the system. It enables the immediate identification of suspicious transactions, facilitating quick responses to potential fraud.

- **Event-driven triggers**: Dynamics 365 AI can be configured to initiate specific actions or alerts based on certain triggers detected through real-time analytics. This could include unusual account activities or transactions that deviate markedly from a customer's usual pattern.

Incorporating external insights

Integration with external data sources provides a richer context for anomaly detection, enhancing Dynamics 365 AI's native analytics:

- **Enriching the anomaly detector**: Copilot's anomaly detector isn't isolated; it craves diversity. External insights enhance its features. They reveal stories of both normalcy and abnormality. Here are some examples:

  - **Financial fraud detection**: Copilot learns from external fraud databases. It identifies unusual spending patterns, sudden account access from foreign IPs, or irregular transaction amounts.

  - **Health monitoring**: Copilot integrates with wearable devices. It detects anomalies in heart rate, sleep patterns, or glucose levels.

  - **Supply chain optimization**: Copilot feasts on external logistics data. It spots deviations in delivery times, inventory levels, or supplier performance.

  By accessing external databases, public records, and online behaviors, Dynamics 365 AI can enrich its analysis, offering a more rounded view of transactions and behaviors.

- **The search for context:** Copilot values context highly and actively seeks external insights

  These insights can come from various sources:

  - **Threat intelligence feeds**: Copilot taps into external threat intelligence feeds. It learns about emerging attack vectors, malicious IPs, and suspicious domains.

- **Industry-specific data**: Copilot craves industry-specific knowledge. For finance, it seeks stock market trends; for healthcare, it looks for medical breakthroughs.

- **User behavior patterns**: Copilot observes user behavior across platforms. It learns from social media interactions, browsing history, and transactional data.

Collaborative platforms and consortiums allow for the cross-industry sharing of fraud signatures and patterns, amplifying Dynamics 365 AI's capability to recognize emerging fraud schemes.

Navigating challenges with precision

Implementing advanced analytics for fraud detection is not without its challenges. Dynamics 365 AI navigates these with precision by enacting the following:

- **Balancing false positives**: Sophisticated algorithms minimize false positives, ensuring that legitimate transactions are not unduly flagged, which could disrupt customer experience.

- **Ensuring data privacy**: Dynamics 365 AI adheres to stringent data privacy regulations, ensuring that the pursuit of fraud detection does not compromise customer confidentiality.

In harnessing advanced analytics for identifying anomalies and patterns, Dynamics 365 AI equips organizations with the tools necessary for proactive fraud detection and prevention. This comprehensive approach not only aids in safeguarding financial and reputational assets but also enhances trust and reliability in digital transactions. As these technologies continue to evolve, Dynamics 365 AI remains at the forefront of innovation, setting new standards in the fight against fraud.

Leveraging Dynamics 365 AI for real-time fraud monitoring and mitigation

The dynamic landscape of digital transactions necessitates a vigilant and responsive approach to fraud detection and mitigation. Dynamics 365 AI rises to this challenge by offering comprehensive solutions for real-time fraud monitoring and mitigation, harnessing the full spectrum of AI capabilities to protect organizations from potential financial and reputational harm. This section delves into the strategies and technologies that enable Dynamics 365 AI to provide immediate fraud detection and take proactive measures to mitigate risks.

Real-time fraud monitoring capabilities

At the core of Dynamics 365 AI's fraud protection strategy is its real-time monitoring capability, which scrutinizes every transaction as it occurs, ensuring the immediate detection of suspicious activities.

- **Continuous transaction analysis**: Dynamics 365 AI employs continuous transaction analysis to monitor the flow of data across business processes. This involves the use of AI models to evaluate transactions against known fraud indicators and historical patterns, flagging anomalies as they arise.

- **Behavioral biometrics**: By incorporating behavioral biometrics, Dynamics 365 AI can detect fraud by analyzing user interactions with systems and applications. This includes assessing keystroke dynamics, mouse movements, and navigation patterns, which can reveal impersonation attempts or unauthorized account access.

Automated alerts and immediate mitigation

The swift identification of potential fraud triggers sets in motion automated alerts, allowing for rapid responses that mitigate risks before they escalate. By promptly detecting anomalies and notifying relevant stakeholders, organizations can proactively safeguard their assets and maintain operational resilience.

- **Configurable alert systems**: Dynamics 365 AI allows organizations to configure custom alert thresholds and parameters, ensuring that alerts are meaningful and actionable. This customization ensures that security teams receive notifications for genuinely suspicious activities, tailored to the specific risk profile of the organization.

- **Automated risk mitigation workflows**: Upon detection of potential fraud, Dynamics 365 AI can initiate predefined workflows to mitigate risks. This might include temporarily suspending transactions, locking user accounts, or initiating additional authentication processes, all automated based on the severity and nature of the detected anomaly.

Adaptive learning for evolving threats

Dynamics 365 AI incorporates a critical feature: adaptive learning. This capability ensures that the system continually evolves in response to emerging threats. By dynamically adjusting its detection algorithms, Dynamics 365 AI remains agile and effective, safeguarding against ever-changing fraudulent activities.

- **Machine learning model updates**: Dynamics 365 AI continuously updates its machine learning models with new data, enabling the system to adapt to emerging fraud tactics and refine its detection algorithms over time.

- **Feedback loops for continuous improvement**: By incorporating feedback from fraud investigations and user reports, Dynamics 365 AI fine-tunes its detection mechanisms, ensuring that the system becomes increasingly effective at identifying and mitigating fraud.

In conclusion, leveraging Dynamics 365 AI for real-time fraud monitoring and mitigation provides organizations with a powerful tool to protect against fraudulent activities. By combining continuous transaction analysis, behavioral biometrics, automated alerts, and adaptive learning, Dynamics 365 AI offers a comprehensive and evolving solution that keeps pace with the ever-changing landscape of fraud. This proactive and intelligent approach ensures that organizations can maintain the integrity of their operations and foster trust among their customers and partners.

Case studies and success stories in fraud protection insights

In the dynamic landscape of fraud prevention, real-world case studies and success stories provide invaluable insights. These narratives illuminate effective strategies, innovative approaches, and lessons learned in the battle against fraudulent activities. Let's delve into these compelling stories where organizations have triumphed over threats and safeguarded their assets.

Case study 1 – Global e-commerce platform enhances security with Dynamics 365 AI

Background: A leading e-commerce platform faced escalating challenges with credit card fraud and account takeovers, threatening customer trust and financial integrity. The platform processed millions of transactions daily, making manual monitoring infeasible.

Challenge: The primary challenge was detecting fraudulent transactions in real-time across a vast, global user base without impacting the customer experience with false positives.

Solution implementation: The company integrated Dynamics 365 AI to leverage its advanced machine learning algorithms for real-time transaction analysis. The solution was configured to analyze purchasing patterns, login behaviors, and payment histories, creating profiles that could identify deviations indicative of fraud. Dynamics 365 AI's adaptive learning capabilities allowed the system to continuously refine its detection accuracy based on confirmed fraud cases and false alarms.

Outcome: The e-commerce platform saw a 40% reduction in credit card fraud within the first six months of implementation. The solution's real-time analysis and adaptive learning significantly improved the accuracy of fraud detection, reducing false positives by 25% and enhancing customer trust. The platform could also automate risk mitigation actions, such as transaction holds and customer verification processes, further securing transactions against fraud.

Case study 2 – Financial institution prevents loan application fraud

Background: A regional bank experienced a surge in fraudulent loan applications, which often went undetected until after funds were disbursed. Traditional rule-based systems were inadequate in identifying sophisticated fraud schemes.

Challenge: The bank needed a solution capable of analyzing complex patterns across application data and customer histories to identify fraudulent applications before approval.

Solution implementation: Dynamics 365 AI was deployed to scrutinize loan applications using predictive analytics and anomaly detection techniques. The bank utilized Dynamics 365 AI to cross-reference application details with historical data and external databases, flagging inconsistencies and patterns associated with known fraud. The system was also integrated with the bank's existing customer relationship management (CRM) system to provide a comprehensive view of applicants' interactions and behaviors.

Outcome: Implementing Dynamics 365 AI resulted in a 60% decrease in fraudulent loan approvals. The bank benefited from the system's deep learning capabilities, which improved its understanding of evolving fraud tactics. Additionally, the integration with the CRM system enhanced the bank's ability to assess applicant credibility, leading to more informed lending decisions and a reduction in financial losses.

Case study 3 – Healthcare provider targets insurance fraud with Dynamics 365 AI

Background: A healthcare provider was losing significant revenue to insurance fraud, including false claims and phantom billing. The provider's legacy systems were ill-equipped to analyze the vast amounts of claim data for signs of fraudulent activity.

Challenge: The provider needed to identify and investigate suspicious claims quickly without delaying legitimate reimbursements to patients and healthcare professionals.

Solution implementation: The healthcare provider implemented Dynamics 365 AI to apply advanced analytics and machine learning to claims processing. The solution analyzed patterns within claims data, comparing them against typical treatment paths and billing practices to flag anomalies. Dynamics 365 AI also used NLP to review claim narratives for discrepancies or signs of manipulation.

Outcome: The adoption of Dynamics 365 AI led to a 50% improvement in the detection of fraudulent claims. The system's ability to analyze and cross-reference data at scale allowed the healthcare provider to identify and investigate suspicious claims more efficiently. This not only prevented financial losses but also streamlined the claims process, ensuring timely payments for legitimate claims and maintaining patient and provider satisfaction.

These case studies demonstrate the powerful capability of Dynamics 365 AI in combating fraud across various sectors. By leveraging machine learning, predictive analytics, and real-time data analysis, organizations can significantly enhance their fraud detection and prevention strategies, safeguarding their assets and reputation in the increasingly digital and interconnected business landscape.

Summary

Throughout this chapter, we have traversed the landscape of modern fraud protection strategies, diving deep into the sophisticated realm of AI-driven technologies. From the foundational aspects of AI-driven fraud detection and prevention strategies to the nuanced applications of identifying anomalies and leveraging real-time monitoring, the journey has illuminated the vast capabilities and potential of Dynamics 365 AI in safeguarding organizations against the multifarious threats of fraud.

The exploration began with a detailed look at how Dynamics 365 AI employs advanced machine learning algorithms and analytics to dissect and understand patterns and anomalies indicative of fraudulent activities. This technical exploration underscored the importance of leveraging AI to not only detect but also predict and prevent fraudulent transactions and behaviors before they can inflict harm.

Moving forward, the narrative delved into the practical application of these technologies, highlighting the real-time fraud monitoring and mitigation capabilities of Dynamics 365 AI. This discussion showcased the power of immediate detection and response, illustrating how organizations can utilize Dynamics 365 AI to create a vigilant and responsive defense against fraud.

The chapter further enriched this narrative with compelling case studies and success stories, bringing to life the abstract concepts and strategies discussed. These real-world examples demonstrated the tangible benefits of integrating Dynamics 365 AI into fraud protection efforts, showcasing significant reductions in fraudulent activities and financial losses and improved operational efficiencies across various industries, including e-commerce, banking, and healthcare.

In drawing from the insights and strategies outlined in this chapter, it is evident that Dynamics 365 AI offers a comprehensive and dynamic toolkit for fraud protection. Its advanced AI capabilities, including machine learning, predictive analytics, and real-time monitoring, provide organizations with a proactive and intelligent approach to detecting, preventing, and mitigating fraud.

However, the journey doesn't end here. As fraudsters continually evolve their tactics, so too must our strategies and technologies adapt. The continuous learning and adaptation capabilities of Dynamics 365 AI ensure that organizations can stay ahead of these threats, adjusting to new patterns of fraud as they emerge. The integration of Dynamics 365 AI into fraud protection efforts represents not just a technological investment but a strategic commitment to maintaining the integrity and trustworthiness of business operations.

In conclusion, leveraging Dynamics 365 AI for fraud protection is a testament to the power of AI in transforming challenges into opportunities for security, efficiency, and trust. As we look to the future, the lessons learned and strategies developed within this chapter will undoubtedly serve as a valuable resource for organizations aiming to fortify their defenses against the ever-present threat of fraud. The journey towards comprehensive fraud protection is ongoing, and Dynamics 365 AI stands as a pivotal ally in navigating this complex terrain, ensuring that businesses can operate with confidence in a digitally connected world. In our exploration of fraud protection, we've delved into the intricacies of safeguarding against deceptive practices. Now, let's pivot our focus toward the exciting advancements and trends that await us in the realm of Dynamics 365 AI.

Questions

1. How does Dynamics 365 AI use machine learning algorithms for fraud detection?

2. What role does real-time monitoring play in Dynamics 365 AI's fraud protection capabilities?

3. How do advanced analytics contribute to identifying anomalies and patterns in fraud detection?

4. Can you describe a real-world application of Dynamics 365 AI in combating fraud based on the case studies presented?

5. What are some of the challenges and considerations organizations must navigate when integrating Dynamics 365 AI for fraud protection?

Answers

1. Dynamics 365 AI uses machine learning algorithms to analyze historical transaction data and learn from it, identifying patterns and behaviors indicative of fraud. These algorithms can distinguish between normal and suspicious activities by continuously refining their detection capabilities based on new data, thereby predicting and preventing potential fraudulent transactions.

2. Real-time monitoring is crucial in Dynamics 365 AI's fraud protection capabilities as it allows for the immediate detection of suspicious activities. By analyzing transactions and behaviors as they occur, Dynamics 365 AI can trigger instant alerts and initiate automated risk mitigation workflows, effectively preventing fraud before it can cause significant damage.

3. Advanced analytics in Dynamics 365 AI contribute to fraud detection by employing statistical analysis and predictive modeling to scrutinize complex datasets for outliers and suspicious patterns. These analytics tools can process vast amounts of data to uncover subtle signs of fraudulent activities that might not be evident through traditional analysis methods.

4. One real-world application of Dynamics 365 AI in combating fraud is seen in a global e-commerce platform that faced challenges with credit card fraud. By integrating Dynamics 365 AI, the platform leveraged machine learning algorithms for real-time transaction analysis, resulting in a 40% reduction in credit card fraud and a significant decrease in false positives, thereby enhancing customer trust and operational efficiency.

5. When integrating Dynamics 365 AI for fraud protection, organizations must navigate challenges such as ensuring data privacy, managing the risk of false positives, and maintaining the accuracy of AI models. It's crucial to balance security measures with customer experience, continuously update and refine AI models to adapt to new fraud tactics and comply with regulatory requirements to protect sensitive customer data effectively.

Part 4:
Looking Ahead

In this concluding part of the book, we venture into the future, exploring the forthcoming trends and developments poised to shape the landscape of Dynamics 365 AI. *Chapter 11* serves as a forward-looking compass, guiding you through the emerging technologies and innovations that will further elevate the capabilities of Dynamics 365 AI. This chapter is dedicated to anticipating the evolution of AI in the business domain, highlighting how advancements will integrate with and expand upon the current functionalities of Dynamics 365 AI. Aimed at professionals who are keen to stay ahead of the curve, this part offers a visionary perspective on the potential shifts and breakthroughs in AI technology. It provides a foundation for strategic thinking and planning, ensuring that businesses are well-prepared to adapt and thrive in the dynamic future of AI-enhanced operations. Through this exploration, you will gain insights into the ongoing journey of AI in business, setting the stage for continuous innovation and success in the era of intelligent technology.

The chapter comprising this Part is titled:

- *Chapter 11, Future Trends and Developments in Dynamics 365 AI*

11

Future Trends and Developments in Dynamics 365 AI

In this chapter, we'll embark on an insightful exploration of the evolving dynamics of AI within the framework of Dynamics 365, Microsoft's comprehensive suite of business applications. This chapter is dedicated to uncovering the next wave of AI innovations that promise to significantly enhance how businesses derive insights, streamline operations, and engage with customers through Dynamics 365. We will dissect the latest trends in AI that are set to revolutionize business intelligence, delve into Microsoft's future vision and the upcoming functionalities for Dynamics 365 AI, and broaden our perspective so that it includes the wider technological advancements in AI that could redefine the platform's capabilities.

This chapter begins by examining the cutting-edge AI trends that are poised to transform business intelligence processes. We will delve into the intricacies of predictive analytics, which is refining its ability to anticipate future business outcomes, and **natural language processing** (**NLP**), which is improving interactions with textual data. This segment aims to illuminate the advancements that will empower businesses to extract more profound insights, facilitating sharper decision-making and strategic foresight.

Next, we'll turn our attention to Microsoft's strategic roadmap for Dynamics 365 AI, providing a detailed look at the anticipated features and enhancements. This portion aims to offer businesses a glimpse into the future capabilities of the platform, enabling them to strategize how they can utilize these forthcoming enhancements to foster innovation and efficiency within their processes.

Furthermore, this chapter expands to consider major advancements in AI technology and their potential impact on Dynamics 365 AI. This includes an exploration of groundbreaking developments, such as quantum computing's role in expediting data analysis, and the ethical implications of integrating increasingly autonomous AI into business decisions. Understanding these broader technological shifts will equip businesses to navigate future challenges and opportunities, ensuring they remain agile in a rapidly changing digital ecosystem.

By providing a detailed exploration of these topics, this chapter aims to furnish you with a thorough understanding of the imminent trends and developments shaping the future of Dynamics 365 AI. Armed with this knowledge, organizations can prepare to leverage the expanding capabilities of AI, positioning themselves at the forefront of digital transformation and securing a competitive edge in the digital era.

Here is a list of topics that will be covered in this chapter:

- Emerging trends in AI for business insights
- Microsoft's roadmap for Dynamics 365 AI—anticipated developments and features
- Exploring advancements in AI technologies and their implications for Dynamics 365 AI

Emerging trends in AI for business insights

The realm of AI is undergoing rapid evolution, pushing the boundaries of what's possible in leveraging data for strategic business insights. As AI becomes more embedded in Dynamics 365 and similar platforms, several key trends are emerging, each with the potential to dramatically transform how businesses understand their operations, customers, and markets.

AI and machine learning sophistication

The sophistication of AI and machine learning algorithms is increasing, allowing for more nuanced and accurate business insights. Advanced models can now process unstructured data—such as text, images, and voice—in real time, offering a richer, more comprehensive analysis. For Dynamics 365 AI, this means enhanced customer service chatbots that understand and react to user sentiment or inventory systems that predict stock levels with high precision based on a multitude of factors, from seasonal demand fluctuations to global supply chain disruptions.

Predictive analytics and forecasting

Predictive analytics is moving from basic trend analysis to complex, multi-variable forecasting models. These models leverage vast datasets to forecast future business conditions, customer behaviors, and market trends with unprecedented accuracy. In Dynamics 365 AI, predictive analytics can identify potential sales opportunities, anticipate customer churn, and optimize marketing strategies, all of which contribute to more informed decision-making.

Automated AI (AutoML) and no-code AI solutions

The rise of automated AI and no-code AI solutions is democratizing access to advanced analytics. This trend is particularly relevant for businesses looking to implement AI without extensive technical expertise. Dynamics 365 AI benefits from this trend by offering pre-built AI models and user-friendly interfaces that allow business analysts and decision-makers to create custom AI solutions for their specific needs, without deep programming knowledge.

AI-driven NLP

NLP technologies are becoming more advanced, enabling machines to understand human language with greater context and accuracy. This advancement is evident in Dynamics 365 AI through enhanced customer interaction tools and more sophisticated data analysis capabilities. Businesses can leverage NLP to analyze customer feedback across various channels, extract valuable insights from social media sentiment, and automate responses to customer inquiries, all in a more human-like manner.

Integration of AI across business processes

AI is becoming more seamlessly integrated across entire business ecosystems, breaking down silos between departments and data sources. This holistic approach enables comprehensive insights that consider all aspects of the business. Dynamics 365 AI facilitates this integration by connecting disparate data sources—CRM, ERP, HR systems, and more—allowing AI models to analyze data across the business and provide insights that are more strategic and actionable.

Ethical AI and bias mitigation

As AI takes on more significant roles in business decision-making, ethical considerations and bias mitigation are becoming paramount. There's a growing focus on developing AI technologies that are transparent, explainable, and free of inherent biases. For Dynamics 365 AI, this means ensuring that AI models are trained on diverse datasets and regularly audited for bias, ensuring that the insights they provide are equitable and reflective of broader societal values.

Edge AI for real-time insights

The emergence of edge AI—where AI computations are performed on local devices rather than centralized servers—promises to speed up the processing of business insights significantly. For Dynamics 365 users, edge AI can enable real-time analytics for mobile sales forces, field service technicians, and retail store managers, providing instant insights without the need for constant connectivity to cloud-based systems.

These emerging trends underscore a future where AI is not just an adjunct to business operations but a core component driving strategic decisions and operational efficiencies. As Dynamics 365 AI and similar platforms evolve to incorporate these advancements, businesses stand to gain unprecedented insights into their operations, empowering them to make more informed, strategic decisions in an ever-changing market landscape.

Microsoft's roadmap for Dynamics 365 AI – anticipated developments and features

As we look toward the future of Dynamics 365 AI, Microsoft is expected to continue its trajectory of integrating advanced AI and machine learning capabilities across its suite of business applications. The roadmap for Dynamics 365 AI encompasses a range of enhancements aimed at making AI more accessible, actionable, and integrated into the fabric of business operations. In this section, we'll look at several anticipated developments and features that could shape the next stages of Dynamics 365 AI.

Enhanced AI models and analytics

Microsoft is expected to further refine and expand its collection of AI models within Dynamics 365, introducing more sophisticated analytics capabilities. This could include more advanced predictive analytics models for forecasting sales trends, customer behavior, and supply chain disruptions. Enhanced AI models might also offer deeper insights into data with minimal setup, enabling businesses to leverage AI-driven analytics with greater ease.

Seamless integration across the Dynamics 365 suite

A key focus of Microsoft's roadmap is likely to be the seamless integration of AI capabilities across the entire Dynamics 365 suite, including finance, supply chain management, sales, and customer service. This integration could allow for unified insights across departments, enabling a more holistic view of business operations and opportunities for cross-functional optimization.

Expanded no-code AI capabilities

To democratize access to AI, Microsoft is anticipated to expand its no-code and low-code AI capabilities within Dynamics 365. This might involve more intuitive interfaces for building custom AI models, as well as expanded tools and templates that allow non-technical users to implement AI-driven solutions tailored to their specific business needs.

Advanced NLP for customer insights

The roadmap for Dynamics 365 AI is expected to include significant advancements in NLP. These improvements could enhance the platform's ability to analyze customer sentiment, intent, and feedback across various channels, providing businesses with deeper customer insights and enabling more personalized customer experiences.

Real-time AI processing at the edge

Acknowledging the growing need for real-time data processing, Microsoft may focus on enhancing the capabilities of Dynamics 365 AI for edge computing. This would allow businesses to leverage AI insights in real time, even in bandwidth-constrained environments, making AI-driven decisions more accessible across all operational contexts.

Ethical AI and governance

As AI becomes more central to business operations, ethical considerations and governance are expected to be a significant focus. Future developments in Dynamics 365 AI could include built-in tools for monitoring AI model fairness, detecting biases, and ensuring compliance with regulatory standards, thereby promoting responsible use of AI.

AI-powered automation and robotic process automation (RPA) enhancements

RPA within Dynamics 365 AI is poised for further enhancements, with AI-powered automation capabilities becoming more sophisticated. This could include smarter bots capable of handling complex tasks and workflows, reducing the need for manual intervention, and streamlining business processes.

Industry-specific AI solutions

Recognizing the unique needs of different industries, Microsoft's roadmap for Dynamics 365 AI is likely to feature the development of industry-specific AI solutions. These solutions would address the particular challenges and opportunities of sectors, such as healthcare, retail, manufacturing, and finance, providing tailored AI insights and functionalities.

As Dynamics 365 AI continues to evolve, these anticipated features and developments represent Microsoft's commitment to empowering businesses with the tools they need to harness AI effectively. By staying informed about these upcoming enhancements, organizations can better prepare to leverage the latest in AI technology to drive innovation, efficiency, and growth.

Exploring advancements in AI technologies and their implications for Dynamics 365 AI

As we delve deeper into the technological revolution sweeping across the digital landscape, it becomes clear that the advancements in AI are not just reshaping our present but are also intricately crafting the future of business operations and strategies. Dynamics 365 AI, standing at the confluence of innovation and practicality, is poised to significantly benefit from these advancements, transforming how businesses interact with their data, engage with customers, and streamline operations. This section explores the cutting-edge developments in AI technologies and their potential implications for Dynamics 365 AI.

Federated learning – a new paradigm in data privacy and AI

Federated learning represents a seismic shift in how AI models are trained, focusing on privacy and data security. By allowing AI models to learn from decentralized data sources without needing to transfer the data to a central server, federated learning opens new avenues for Dynamics 365 AI applications in sectors where data privacy is paramount, such as healthcare and finance. This approach not only enhances privacy but also enables more personalized AI experiences by leveraging data directly from the devices and interactions closest to the end users.

AI and the Internet of Things (IoT) – bridging the physical and digital worlds

The integration of AI with IoT technologies heralds a new era of interconnectedness, where real-world data becomes a cornerstone of business insights. For Dynamics 365 AI, this integration means harnessing real-time data from sensors and devices across the supply chain, retail environments, and production floors. The implications are profound, from predictive maintenance and enhanced supply chain visibility to personalized retail experiences based on real-time customer behaviors.

Quantum computing – supercharging AI's analytical capabilities

Quantum computing promises to revolutionize the computational power available for AI, offering the ability to process complex problems and datasets far beyond the reach of classical computers. For Dynamics 365 AI, quantum computing could supercharge analytics capabilities, making it feasible to solve intricate optimization problems, simulate complex systems for product development, and analyze vast datasets for insights in seconds. This leap in computational power could drastically reduce the time needed for data processing and model training, opening up new possibilities for real-time analytics and decision-making.

Explainable AI (XAI) – enhancing transparency and trust

As AI becomes more prevalent in decision-making processes, the demand for transparency and understanding of how AI models arrive at their conclusions has led to the emergence of XAI. For Dynamics 365 AI, XAI could transform customer trust and compliance by providing clear, understandable explanations for AI-driven decisions. This is particularly crucial in industries such as finance and healthcare, where decisions need to be both accurate and transparent. XAI can help businesses build trust with their customers and stakeholders by making AI's decision-making processes more transparent and accountable.

Generative pre-trained transformers (GPT) and advanced NLP – revolutionizing customer interactions

The advancements in GPT and other NLP technologies are set to redefine customer service and engagement. Dynamics 365 AI can leverage these technologies to create more sophisticated, conversational AI agents capable of understanding and generating human-like responses. This leap in NLP capabilities means businesses can provide more nuanced, context-aware customer service, automate complex interactions, and generate content at scale, enhancing customer engagement and satisfaction.

AI ethics and governance – shaping a responsible future

With great power comes great responsibility. The advancements in AI technologies bring the critical importance of ethics and governance in AI deployment to the fore. For Dynamics 365 AI, embedding ethical AI practices and governance frameworks is essential to ensure that AI solutions are fair, unbiased, and aligned with societal values. This includes developing AI models that are transparent, explainable, and free from discriminatory biases, ensuring that AI-driven decisions promote equity and fairness.

These advancements in AI technologies not only herald a new dawn of possibilities for Dynamics 365 AI but also underscore the need for businesses to adapt, innovate, and consider the broader implications of AI integration. As Dynamics 365 AI continues to evolve, leveraging these technologies responsibly and effectively will be key to unlocking their transformative potential, driving business growth, and shaping a future where AI enhances every facet of the business landscape.

Summary

In this chapter, we traversed a landscape brimming with potential and innovation. From emerging trends that are reshaping the realm of AI in business insights to the anticipated advancements and their profound implications for Dynamics 365 AI, it's clear that we are on the cusp of a transformative era in business technology.

The journey began with an in-depth look at the emerging trends in AI for business insights, highlighting how advancements such as predictive analytics, automated AI, and sophisticated natural language processing are set to enhance the depth and breadth of insights businesses can derive from their data. These trends not only promise to streamline operations and optimize customer engagements but also to unlock new opportunities for growth and innovation within the Dynamics 365 AI ecosystem.

Moving forward, we delved into Microsoft's roadmap for Dynamics 365 AI, examining the upcoming features poised to elevate the platform's capabilities. This forward-looking perspective underscored Microsoft's commitment to integrating cutting-edge AI technologies into Dynamics 365, ensuring that businesses equipped with this platform remain at the forefront of digital transformation.

The final section broadened our view to consider the broader advancements in AI technologies and their potential to revolutionize Dynamics 365 AI. From quantum computing's potential to process data at unprecedented speeds to the ethical considerations of deploying AI in decision-making processes, it's evident that the future of Dynamics 365 AI is intertwined with the evolution of AI at large. These advancements are not just technical enhancements; they represent a shift toward more intelligent, responsive, and adaptable business solutions.

In conclusion, the future of Dynamics 365 AI is one of immense promise and potential. As AI technologies continue to evolve, Dynamics 365 AI is set to become even more integral to how businesses operate, make decisions, and engage with their customers. The implications of these advancements extend beyond mere operational efficiency or improved customer service; they touch on the very way businesses think about and interact with data, technology, and their customers.

As we look to the future, organizations that embrace these trends and prepare for the integration of upcoming features and advancements within their Dynamics 365 AI deployments will be well-positioned to lead in their respective industries. The journey into the future of Dynamics 365 AI is one of continuous learning, adaptation, and innovation, promising to unlock new levels of insight, efficiency, and opportunity for businesses ready to embark on this transformative path.

Questions

1. What emerging AI trend in business insights focuses on enhancing the way businesses understand and interact with textual data, and how does it benefit Dynamics 365 AI?

2. How does predictive analytics within Dynamics 365 AI contribute to strategic decision-making for businesses?

3. What is the significance of automated AI (AutoML) and no-code AI solutions in the context of Dynamics 365 AI?

4. Discuss the role of quantum computing in the future of Dynamics 365 AI and its potential impact on data processing.

5. What are the ethical considerations businesses must keep in mind when deploying AI in decision-making processes, particularly in the use of Dynamics 365 AI?

Answers

1. The emerging AI trend that focuses on enhancing businesses' interaction with textual data is advanced NLP. It benefits Dynamics 365 AI by improving customer service chatbots' understanding and response to user sentiments and enabling more sophisticated data analysis capabilities, allowing for deeper insights into customer feedback and inquiries.

2. Predictive analytics within Dynamics 365 AI contributes to strategic decision-making by leveraging vast datasets to forecast future business conditions, customer behaviors, and market trends with unprecedented accuracy. This enables businesses to identify potential sales opportunities, anticipate customer churn, and optimize marketing strategies, thereby making more informed and strategic decisions.

3. The significance of automated AI (AutoML) and no-code AI solutions in Dynamics 365 AI lies in democratizing access to advanced analytics. These tools allow business analysts and decision-makers to create custom AI solutions for specific needs without deep programming knowledge, significantly lowering the barrier to implementing AI and enabling businesses to harness AI capabilities more easily for enhanced insights and operations.

4. Quantum computing's role in the future of Dynamics 365 AI is to revolutionize data processing capabilities. Its potential impact includes processing complex datasets at speeds previously unattainable, enabling Dynamics 365 AI to analyze more data in less time and with greater depth. This could lead to more accurate models, faster insights, and the ability to solve complex problems that are currently beyond reach, significantly enhancing business intelligence and operational efficiency.

5. When deploying AI in decision-making processes using Dynamics 365 AI, businesses must consider ethical aspects such as transparency, accountability, and bias mitigation. Ensuring that AI models are transparent and their decisions can be explained is crucial for maintaining trust. Businesses must also be accountable for the AI's decisions and actively work to identify and mitigate any biases in AI models to ensure fair and equitable outcomes for all stakeholders.

Index

packtpub.com

Subscribe to our online digital library for full access to over 7,000 books and videos, as well as industry leading tools to help you plan your personal development and advance your career. For more information, please visit our website.

Why subscribe?

- Spend less time learning and more time coding with practical eBooks and Videos from over 4,000 industry professionals

- Improve your learning with Skill Plans built especially for you

- Get a free eBook or video every month

- Fully searchable for easy access to vital information

- Copy and paste, print, and bookmark content

Did you know that Packt offers eBook versions of every book published, with PDF and ePub files available? You can upgrade to the eBook version at packtpub.com and as a print book customer, you are entitled to a discount on the eBook copy. Get in touch with us at customercare@packtpub.com for more details.

At www.packtpub.com, you can also read a collection of free technical articles, sign up for a range of free newsletters, and receive exclusive discounts and offers on Packt books and eBooks.

Other Books You May Enjoy

If you enjoyed this book, you may be interested in these other books by Packt:

Administrating Microsoft Dynamics 365 Business Central Online

Andrey Baludin

ISBN: 978-1-80323-480-9

- Manage different Business Central environments, their statuses, and updates, and create new environments
- Understand how to deploy a SaaS environment from a backup
- Analyze environment telemetry and its operation, and discover how to set up extended telemetry with Application Insights
- Explore how to get information about tenant capacity limits and their usage of resources
- Set up cloud migration and move your data from on-premise to SaaS
- Automate administration and migration processes with APIs

Extending Dynamics 365 Finance and Operations Apps with Power Platform

Adrià Ariste Santacreu

ISBN: 978-1-80181-159-0

- Get to grips with integrating Dynamics 365 F&O with Dataverse
- Discover the benefits of using Power Automate with Dynamics 365 F&O
- Understand Power Apps as a means to extend the functionality of Dynamics 365 F&O
- Build your skills to implement Azure Data Lake Storage for Power BI reporting
- Explore AI Builder and its integration with Power Automate Flows and Power Apps
- Gain insights into environment management, governance, and application lifecycle management (ALM) for Dataverse and the Power Platform

Packt is searching for authors like you

If you're interested in becoming an author for Packt, please visit `authors.packtpub.com` and apply today. We have worked with thousands of developers and tech professionals, just like you, to help them share their insight with the global tech community. You can make a general application, apply for a specific hot topic that we are recruiting an author for, or submit your own idea.

Share Your Thoughts

Now you've finished *Microsoft Dynamics 365 AI for Business Insights*, we'd love to hear your thoughts! Scan the QR code below to go straight to the Amazon review page for this book and share your feedback or leave a review on the site that you purchased it from.

https://packt.link/r/180181094X

Your review is important to us and the tech community and will help us make sure we're delivering excellent quality content.

Download a free PDF copy of this book

Thanks for purchasing this book!

Do you like to read on the go but are unable to carry your print books everywhere?

Is your eBook purchase not compatible with the device of your choice?

Don't worry, now with every Packt book you get a DRM-free PDF version of that book at no cost.

Read anywhere, any place, on any device. Search, copy, and paste code from your favorite technical books directly into your application.

The perks don't stop there, you can get exclusive access to discounts, newsletters, and great free content in your inbox daily

Follow these simple steps to get the benefits:

1. Scan the QR code or visit the link below

https://packt.link/free-ebook/978-1-80181-094-4

2. Submit your proof of purchase

3. That's it! We'll send your free PDF and other benefits to your email directly

www.ingramcontent.com/pod-product-compliance
Lightning Source LLC
Chambersburg PA
CBHW080531060326
40690CB00022B/5093